The NEW Creature

Discover the New Life Within

FATAI KASALI

THE NEW CREATURE

Copyright © 2014 Fatai Kasali

The author reserves all right. Unless otherwise stated all scripture quotations are taken from the Authorised King James Version of the Bible.

No part of this publication maybe reproduced, stored in a retrieval system, or transmitted, in any form or by any means, electronic, mechanical, photocopying, recording or otherwise without the prior permission of Glory Publishing.

Published in the United Kingdom by Glory Publishing.

ISBN: 978-0-9926138-1-5

ACKNOWLEDGEMENTS

To God be the glory for the grace to write this new book. I am very grateful to the almighty God for giving me inspiration and all necessary resources needed to make this book a reality.

I acknowledge, with an immense appreciation, the works of the following people in editing this book: Mr Mayowa Peters, Mr Adeyemi Adeniyi, Mr Adeyemi Bukola, and Ms Ehime Ayeni.

I acknowledge the diverse support from my wonderful family towards the writing of this book. My wife, Felicia Ebunlomo, and my two sons, Daniel and David, have made my life glorious. I thank the almighty God for blessing me with such a wonderful family.

To all the members of the Redeemed Christian Church of God, Glory of God Parish, Bristol, thanks for being there for me and my family.

INTRODUCTION

2 Corinthians 5:17
Therefore if any man be in Christ, he is a new creature: old things are passed away; behold, all things are become new.

THE ABOVE BIBLE VERSE indicates that Christians are new creatures. They have been regenerated. If there could be new, then, there must be old. Though, we are now new creatures, it is imperative that we don't totally forget how the old looks like, otherwise we may drift into the old without knowing.

This book compares the old and the new life. It exposes the lifestyle of a natural man yet to be born-again. There are many Christians that claim that they are new creatures but a close examination of their lifestyle indicates otherwise. Though, they claim to be born-again, they still live the life they used to live before giving their lives to Jesus Christ.

As a new creature, a different lifestyle is expected of you. You are to apply the principles of the kingdom of God in every area of your life. When you become a new creature, you receive divine knowledge that enables you deny the devil any opportunity to lure you into the practice of the former things. The devil does not care if you claim that you are a new creature as long as you practise the old lifestyle. Being a new creature is not only in confession but also in daily living.

CONTENTS

1 OUR **DESIRES** HAVE CHANGED 9

2 OUR **HOPE** HAS CHANGED 23

3 OUR **YOKE** HAS CHANGED 43

4 OUR **FEAR** HAS CHANGED 53

5 OUR **HEARTS** HAVE CHANGED 73

6 OUR **HERITAGE** HAS CHANGED 109

7 OUR **LIVES** HAVE CHANGED 125

8 OUR **NEW NAMES** IN PRAYER 139

OUR **DESIRES** HAVE CHANGED

OUR DESIRES MANIFEST IN those things that we pursue today. The things we seek are reflections of our desires. Desires drive. In the old life, before we met Jesus, we used to pursue different desires which are contrary to those of the kingdom of God. Examples of things that we pursued in the old life are:

A.   REVENGE

This is the act of inflicting punishment on others due to the offence committed against us. The old man seeks and pursues revenge to satisfy himself that he has not been cheated and taken advantage of. In **2 Samuel 13:13-30**, Absalom organised a party to seek revenge for the offence committed by his brother, Amnon, against his sister, Tamar. This, he did two years after the offence had been committed. Absalom organised the killing of Amnon.

A new creature of the Lord Jesus will not desire vengeance because he has been regenerated. If you pursue revenge, your salvation is questionable. **Romans 12:17-19** was written to the new creatures of God, admonishing them not to seek revenge. This is because revenge will cause you to do evil and this will position you for the accusation of the enemy. *Proverbs 24:29* warn the new creatures of God not to pay evil for evil. A new creature of God does only good and there is no evil in him.

In *Matthew 5:39*, Jesus commanded the new creatures of God not to fight an evil person back. The command implies that we should not allow an evil man to influence us to do like him. When you refuse to revenge, you have indirectly created a position for God in the matter. You then position God to fight for you since you have decided not to fight for yourself. The judgement of God is sweet. It gives comfort to the offended.

Don't be tempted to think that because the person that offended you would get away with it, you need to punish him. In reality, no one will get away with anything in this world because it is written in *Genesis 8:22* that there will always be a time of sowing and reaping. Everyone will reap what they have sown in this world. Whoever makes you cry shall one day be made to cry. Let God take vengeance. May God give you enough patience not to fight for yourself but to allow Him do the fighting for you in Jesus name.

B.　WORLDLY PLEASURES

In the old life, we sought worldly pleasures because they satisfied our flesh. They make our flesh feel good and fat. In the old life, we derived satisfaction from eating, drinking, sleeping and feeding on the provisions the world can provide for us. We lived like people that would never die. The old man never thought of another life because he is not just myopic but also blind.

No wonder there are a lot of people who have died before they eventually die physically. There are so many walking corpses in our world today. In *Luke 15:13-16*, the prodigal son demanded his inheritance prematurely and went to a far country to waste it. He entered into the world of pleasure. The world promised him that with his inheritance in his hands, he would never experience pains and sorrow. Soon, he discovered that he had been deceived.

There is nothing wrong in living in a far country but we must never forget home because one day, we have to return home either voluntarily or by force. Heaven is the home of new creatures and this world is our foreign land. Whether we like it or not, one day we shall have to return home. Hence, we need to constantly think of home as we transact our businesses in this far place we stay in presently.

In *2 Timothy 4:10*, Paul wrote to Timothy that Demas had forsaken him because he loved this world. The old man loves this world and all its pleasures but soon, he will be disappointed. In *James 4:3*, it is written that people could not receive answers to their prayers because their desire was on worldly pleasures. Why did you ask from God what you asked for? Do you pursue the pleasures of this world or that of heaven? It is good to enjoy life but not at the detriment of making heaven. When last did you put aside food, drink, sleep and certain enjoyment in order to develop yourself spiritually?

May God pour His grace upon your life to enable you become heaven-focused in all that you do in Jesus 'name.

C. POSSESSING THE POSSESSIONS OF ANOTHER MAN

The old man is wicked and greedy. He is self-seeking. It is the possessions of another man that always interest the old man. He desires the blessings of another man. He is full of covetousness.

In *1 King 21:1-15*, Ahab desired the land of Naboth and he started to scheme in order to possess it. He succeeded, but with divine curses placed upon him and his entire home. The old man is never satisfied with God's provisions. He wants the gift of another man. He wants the position of another man. He wants the wife of another man. He wants the prosperity of another man. He wants the ministry of another man. He believes that the possession of another man is far better than his own.

In *2 Samuel 11:1-6*, David considered the wife of another man more beautiful than all his wives and he schemed to get her but ended with divine curses upon his life and his home. God told David in *2 Samuel 12*:8 that He would have given him more blessings if what He had given him were little. That is, God has given you at the moment what you actually need for this time. He will give you more when He discovers that there is a need for more in your life. The new creatures live on God provisions. They do not covet what belongs to another man.

In *Hebrews 13:5*, God promises never to leave His children alone. He will supply all their needs. What do you seek today? Do you pursue the possession of another man? If you do, stop it now before it becomes hard for you to stop. In *Philippians 4:19*, Paul stated that God shall supply all your needs. That is, it is God that shall supply all your needs, not you supplying your own needs by hook or by crook. New creatures allow God to supply all their needs. They do not do it by themselves because if they should, they will fall into diverse temptations and sins. The new creatures of God are heaven-focused, not self-focused. After learning a lot of lessons, David discovered another way of getting his needs and he said in *Psalm 121:1-2*, that he would always look unto the heaven where his help comes from God. He also discovered in *Psalm 23* that he has a shepherd that would always supply his needs. Therefore, there is no need to run after another man's possessions since you have a God that manages your life affairs.

It is written in *Micah 2:1-3*, that he that schemes to possess the possession of another man shall fall into divine disaster. May God help you to live a life that attracts blessings and not curses in Jesus name. Amen.

D. VAIN GLORY

The old man is full of pride. He pursues his own glory and not that of his creator. He wants to make a name for himself. He is interested in building fame and honour for himself. In *Genesis 11:1-8*, the people of the earth came together to build a tower with the purpose of making name for themselves. They wanted to make themselves heroes, forgetting that it is God Almighty that makes heroes. They ended up with confusion and shame. Their names were never remembered. God rubbed off their memory from the earth. Are you pursuing the name of God or your own name? In *Daniel 4:30-31*, King Nebuchadnezzar built a kingdom for his name and eventually became an animal. He lost his position of honour until he came to his senses. Are you still building for your own name? If so, you are not yet a new creature. The new creature builds for God because he pursues the name of God. In *1 Samuel 16:30*, Saul demanded honour before the people despite dishonouring the name of God through his disobedience. He was more interested in his own honour and respect. He ended his journey in insanity.

The new creatures pursue the Name of God who wants people that will protect His name. In *2 Samuel 17:36*, David fought Goliath to protect the Name of God. Those who live their lives in protecting the Name of God shall never be forgotten by both God and men; but those who live their lives to build names for themselves shall never be remembered. In *Philippians 2:7-9*, Jesus was given a name that is above all other names because He never pursued His own glory. He never received praise from man and never demanded for honour.

Whatever you are ready to lose for God's sake shall come back to you

Every loss you experienced because of God's Name shall turn out to become your gain. The new creatures of God neither pursue empty glory nor build an empire for themselves. They do not seek human praise. *Philippians 2:3* says let nothing be done in vain glory. That is, let no man pursue or seek his own glory. This instruction is for the new creatures of God. Empty glory never lasts. Those who build for themselves will soon discover that they have built for another man to take over, but those who build for God shall never be forgotten.

Do you want to become a hero? Start building for God now and the world shall never forget you even after you have long gone. May God give you a heart that fears Him always in Jesus name. May God make His grace to be sufficient for you in all situations and give you a heart that pants for Him.

E. SELF–RULE

The old man does not want to subject himself to any government or authority. He wants independent self-government. He hates being ruled by any authority, either of God or of man. The old man's desire is to be independent so that he can live as it pleases him. In **1 Samuel 8:1-9**, the Israelites demanded self-rule from God. They did not want to be ruled by judges appointed by God. They wanted their own king. They wanted their destiny to be determined by themselves and not God.

The old man never subjects himself to any authority. He feels too big to be ruled. In **Psalm 106:14-21**, God accepted the demand of the Israelites for a king but He sent leanness into their souls. God will not rule anyone by force but He will not show His favour to any independent government. Man was created to live under the authority of God because he did not create himself. The new creatures of God shall live under the authority which God has placed them.

In *John 15:16*, Jesus told the disciples that He chose them and not the other way round. He is the master. In the kingdom of God there shall always be one master because any animal with two heads is definitely a monster. Are you under an authority or have you chosen to establish your own? Are you accountable to any man appointed by God or do you give account to yourself? God has established authority in the kingdom of men so that man can account to Him through man. Is there any man that calls you to order if you misbehave or you are just on your own? The new creatures of God function effectively under the human authority God has placed them.

If you claim that you have asked God for independence and He has given it, it may be true, but, when God accepted the independent government the Israelites demanded, He sent leanness to their souls. Check to ascertain if God has not done the same thing to you. Sometimes, God says 'yes' because He does not want to rule you by force. May God grant you a heart of humility in Jesus' name.

Consequences of the old man's desires

The desires pursued by the old man have greater consequences which make a case for the old to die so that the new can thrive. Examples of consequences of the desires of the old man are:

1.   MADNESS OF THE HEART

The old man has many desires. It is written in Ecclesiastes 9:3, that there is madness in the hearts of men. A man of many desires is prone to madness of the heart. Whenever a man is left to himself by God, he enters into insanity. When God departed from the life of Saul, he ran mad - **1 Samuel 16:14**, Saul became like a woman that has no husband; who lives alone and rules herself. During his days of madness, Paul called himself an injurious person (**1 Timothy 1:13-15**). An injurious person oppresses and puts other people to death. He does evil without restraint. If you do evil without restraint, you are not yet a new creature. If you willfully or intentionally pursue that which will destroy you, you are not yet a new creature.

If the Holy-Spirit cannot tame your heart, you are not yet a new creature because madness belongs to the untamed heart. A mad man operates under an evil anointing-he does evil in an extra-ordinary way. Are you mad or normal? Is your heart being tamed by the Holy-Spirit? Do you see yourself well-dressed when you are actually naked?

2. ANXIETY

Many desires produce anxiety. Anxiety comes because you are in control of your life, but a man that has cast all his burdens unto Jesus has no time for anxiety because he knows God is the manager of his destiny.

In *Matthew 6:25*, Jesus encouraged people to stop worrying about their needs and in **1 Peter 5:7**, we are advised to cast all our burdens unto Jesus. Anxiety is a symptom which reveals that a desire is not likely to have its origin in God, because whenever God gives vision he also gives provision. You cannot be anxious about what did not have its root in you, because its fulfilment and realisation will not depend on you. Are you anxious about anything? If so, maybe you are pursuing your own idea and not that of God.

3. PERVERSION

Perversion is to change or twist what was originally good. It means to make a straight thing crooked. So many desires will lead to perversion. **1 Timothy 6:5** says that perversion is a product of a corrupt mind. The mind gets corrupted because the old man has discovered that his so many desires will not be met unless the rules are bent to his favour. If you want to bend the rule in order to achieve your desires, you are a perverse person. You are a twister, making straight things crooked to favour you. **Proverbs 11:3** confirms that perverseness destroys its captive. You must stop bending the rules of the game now before it destroys you. A new creature of God follows the rule of the game because he has integrity to protect.

4. A TREASURY OF EVIL

Matthew 12:33-35 says that an evil man, out of the evil treasure, brings forth an evil thing. The old man has so many desires to please himself and since all these cannot be achieved through a legitimate route, he resorts to evil practices. A plethora of desires will invite so many means of achieving them. This would spring up so many suggestions and ideas that are sinful. If your heart has a treasury of evil, you are not yet a new creature. If you harbour thoughts that embrace scheming and manipulation, you are not yet a new creature. It is time for you to overhaul your heart.

5. FAR FROM GOD

The more your heart is crowded with so many selfish desires, the more you are drawn away from God. It is written in *Isaiah 29:13* that people draw near to God with their lips but are far away from Him in their hearts. When your desire does not originate from God, to pursue it will draw you far away from Him. Are you far from God? How sensitive are you spiritually? Do you realise that an action is a sin after you have committed it? Do you hear the still small voice (*1 Kings 19:12*) when you are about to act wrongly? If not, then you are not yet a new creature because a new creature hears the voice of his creator. So what next if our desire has changed?

Our new desire

The old is dead and the new has come. The point of regeneration announces the dawn of a new era. Our desires are changed. Our pursuits are made new. The new creature now has only one desire to pursue. Gone are the days of so many desires.

> **Matthew 6:33**
> Seek first the kingdom of God and its righteousness, and all these things shall be added unto you.

The new creature now pursues only the kingdom of God in all areas of his life. He pursues kingdom ideas and operations concerning every area of his life and establishes kingdom principles and dominion over every area of his life. He pursues and establishes what God says concerning his marital life, career, ministry, education, health etc. The new creature has discovered the Owner of his life and so he pursues only the will of God concerning every area of his life. He puts aside many desires of his own but embraces those of God.

When the focus is to do the will of God in all things, then we have a single desire to pursue. And when you seek the kingdom of God in all things, all other things you did not pursue will begin to pursue you. When you establish kingdom ideas in your marriage, the fruits of the womb, peace and prosperity which you did not ask for, will flow into your home. Every demonic oppression is automatically destroyed. When you establish kingdom ideas in your career, the promotion and fruitfulness you did not ask for, will start manifesting in your career.

The kingdom of God is here. The new creature establishes the kingdom of God in all areas of his life. This is the only desire he has. It is written in **Romans 14:17** that the kingdom of God is in righteousness, peace and joy in the Holy Spirit. Wherever the kingdom of God is established, there will be righteousness (absence of every manner of evil), peace (divine peace) and joy (caused by the presence of the Almighty God). Those that walk not after the desires of the flesh shall establish the doctrines and dominion of the kingdom of God in every area of their lives.

Benefits of a single desire

When you seek and establish God's kingdom principles and ideas in all areas of your life, you will enjoy the following benefits:

1. FREEDOM FROM FOREIGN KINGDOMS

Daniel 2:44, we see *'And in the days of these kings shall the God of heaven set up a kingdom, which shall never be destroyed: and the kingdom shall not be left to other people, but it shall break in pieces and consume all these kingdoms, and it shall stand for ever.'*

That is, the kingdom of God has the capability to destroy every other fake kingdom. When the kingdom of God is established in your finances, every demonic power including those of the devourer, wastefulness and lack is destroyed. The kingdom of God cannot co-exist with another kingdom. May God establish His kingdom in every area of your life today in Jesus' name.

2. DESIRED CHANGES HAPPEN ON THEIR OWN ACCORD

Because the kingdom of God is in power, the power causes desired change. *'For the kingdom of God is not in word, but in power.'* (***1 Corinthians 4:20***). When you establish the kingdom of God in any area of your life, all the changes you desire get established automatically. The more you bring your life under the dominion of God's kingdom, the more positive changes you will experience. The new creatures desire and seek only the kingdom of God. This is the secret of their peace and boldness. It is because they have a kingdom that cannot be shaken. May God rule in all areas of your life. May God protect your life against any evil invasion in Jesus' name.

2

OUR HOPE HAS CHANGED

HOPE GIVES FOCUS and channels expectations positively in all situations. Hope gives the confidence of a favourable outcome. Your confidence is imbued in your hope. So, though what you expect has not happened yet, you are sure it will happen. It is hope that keeps you going and makes you to continue doing what you do. It is your confidence in the positive end to a thing or situation that keeps your hope alive.

The old man had his own hope before regeneration. He had certain things that gave him the confidence of success in all he did. We shall consider some examples of things we used to put our hope in, before regeneration. This will help us not to fall into the mistake of hoping against hope now that we have become new creatures. We shall also consider what we should put our hope in, as new creatures of God. Examples of things we had put our hope in before regeneration are:

1. RICHES

The old man was confident that the more riches he had, the more assured would be his future and success in life. The temptation of putting hope in riches is so great that men commit unusual evil to acquire it as every man wants the assurance of security. A man without Jesus needs to make effort to secure his future since God is not the manager of his life.

Despite being very rich, Job stated in *Job 31:24* that he had never made riches his hope. He probably discovered that riches have limited assistance to offer in certain matters of life, so he never hoped for deliverance through riches. *Zephaniah 1:18* declares that riches are useless on the day of God's wrath. Riches, no matter how much, cannot provide solace or shelter when calamity comes. *Proverbs 23:5* states that riches do fly away like an eagle towards heaven. When this happens, those that have put their hope in it get disappointed. The new creatures of God should not put their hope and confidence in riches. They should no longer idolise riches because they have been set free indeed. We have been saved not to be ruled by riches but by God. May He give you the grace not to lose your liberty in Christ in Jesus' name.

2. POSITION

Some people put their hope in position because they are confident that it will enable them to succeed in life. Many people strive and struggle to occupy positions of power where they can influence situations to their own benefit. For such people their, position is their god.

Abimelech, the son of Gideon, killed his brothers in order to become king in *Judges 9:5-6*. He wanted the position of authority at any cost because that was where his hope was.

There are so many Abimelechs in our world today. They are very ruthless, desperate and ready to do every kind of evil to gain power because that is where their hope is. That is the way of the old man. The new creatures of God have discovered a better source of hope. It is written in **Psalm 75:6-7**, that exaltation comes from God only.

Those that put their hope in God and not in position shall be exalted to the position of power. Without any struggle, in **Genesis 41:39-41**, Joseph was promoted to the position of power in a foreign land because his hope was in the Lord, not in position. He was given what he did not fight for. God is the genuine promoter and He appoints people into position according to His discretion. Do you want a position of power? Put your hope not in anything but in God and you shall soon rise to power.

3. HUMAN BEINGS

Some people put their hope in fellow human beings. They worship man to receive favour. Unfortunately, they will soon be disappointed.

> **Psalm 146:3**
> Put not your trust in princes, or in the son of man, in whom there is no help.

The reason behind this piece of advice is stated in **Isaiah 2:22**: *'Cease ye from man, whose breath is in his nostrils: for wherein is he to be accounted of?'*

That is, all that makes man is in the breath of his nostrils. Man is frail and short-lived. If your trust for deliverance and salvation is in man, instead of God, you will soon meet with speedy and utter disappointment. Since man is visible, he finds it easier to put his trust in man at the expense of the invisible God. Thus, the nature of man finds it easier to believe in what he could see than what is not visible. If you are still seeking for human support at the expense of that of God, you are not yet a new creature. Man did not save you from your old ways. It was God that delivered you from the power of darkness and in Him your hope should lie.

4. HUMAN WISDOM

Wisdom can be described as the application of knowledge. Some people have gotten a lot of knowledge such that their hope is the application of such knowledge. They have confidence in their knowledge such that they boast of it. But which kind of knowledge? Is it the knowledge of God or of this world?

There is a challenge in *James 3:13-17*: *'Who is a wise man and endued with knowledge among you? Let him show out of a good conversation his works with meekness of wisdom. But if ye have bitter envying and strife in your hearts, glory not, and lie not against the truth. This wisdom descended not from above, but is earthly, sensual, and devilish. For where envying and strife is, there is confusion and every evil Work. But the wisdom that is from above is first pure, then peaceable, gentle, and easy to be entreated, full of mercy and good fruits, without partiality, and without hypocrisy.'*

The knowledge of this world is natural and evil and its application is of the same stock. The people of the world are crafty, not wise. If your hope is in your ability to apply the knowledge you have acquired in this world, you will soon be disappointed. The reason is because only the wisdom of God is supreme. In *Genesis 41:1-8*, all the wise men of Egypt could not interpret the dream of King Pharaoh until Joseph was invited into the matter. God sealed up the heaven and all the wise men of Egypt became foolish.

Are you still boasting of your wisdom? There are many things you will not be able to interpret because you have limited knowledge. Secrets dwell with God and only those he reveals them to will be made wise. There is a wisdom that cannot be limited. There is a wisdom that cannot be frustrated. There is a wisdom that is dynamic. *Ephesians 3:10* describes the wisdom of God as manifold. It is multifarious. It has solutions to all issues. The new creatures of God must embrace the wisdom of God, and not that of this world which will come to nothing.

5. EARTHLY HELP

Some people put their hope in earthly help. They hope that the world they live in is rich enough and has abundant resources that will sustain them in every situation they may find themselves. This is their boast and confidence as is written in *Psalms 20: 7-8*: *'Some trust in chariots, and some in horses: but we will remember the name of the LORD our God. They are brought down and fallen: but we are risen, and stand upright.'*

Chariots and horses are suitable for fighting battles of life. Some have acquired a lot of weapon for self-defence and in this, they put their hope. Some people have built a strong wall of friends and earthly resources around themselves such that they feel secure and safe. Unfortunately they do not realise their vulnerability. With all the weapons and armours of Goliath, only a single stone brought him down in **1 Samuel 17:45-50**. No matter how well you dress yourself for the battles of life there will always be a small hole in the armour. The new creatures of God should trust in the Name of God for victory in the battles of life. Our hope should always be in the deliverance power of God. Are you a new breed of God? If yes, then your hope should not be in the help the world provides. **Except God dresses you for battle, you will always be vulnerable.**

6. PAST ACHIEVEMENTS

There is nothing as deceitful as trusting in your past victory in the face of the battle of the present. Every battle is different. Your past victory was to strengthen your confidence in God, not in yourself. Past achievements do not guarantee future victory. Yesterday is gone and today is different. Every day comes with its own uniqueness.

The natural man will say: 'I have done it before and I will always do it again,' but, the new creature of God will say: 'God has done it before and He will always do it again.' You will always need God. Joshua learnt the lesson that past achievement does not necessarily guarantee future victory in **Joshua 7:1-12**. He went to fight the small village of Ai shortly after his victory against the mighty Jericho. To Joshua, the small village of Ai should not be a challenge; after all, they recently defeated the mighty Jericho. Alas! Joshua and all Israelites were proved wrong. They lost the battle woefully.

Things change quickly and mostly without our knowledge. Joshua and Israel defeated mighty Jericho because God was on their side but they lost the battle against little Ai because God was not involved. The new creatures of God will always win because they always hope in God, not in their past achievements. **Don't be deceived; you can't always win unless God is always on your side.**

7. NUMBER

Number is good. The more people on your side the better is the opportunity for you to win an election. It is about number. Yet, do not be deceived by number and do not put your hope in it as some people do. The natural man seeks for more supporters because he blindly believes that only the number counts. Number is good but it is God that controls where the tide should shift. It is written in **Proverbs 21:1**: *'The king's heart is in the hand of the LORD, as the rivers of water: he turneth it whithersoever he will.'*

God determines where the supporters should go. If God votes for you the whole world will follow suit. Only God voted for Joseph in Egypt and he became the Prime Minister. In **Genesis 41**, King Pharaoh and his people unanimously agreed to make Joseph their Prime Minister. You need God more than number. In **Deuteronomy 20:1**, God instructed the Israelites not to be afraid of battle because of their numerous enemies. He is more than billions of enemies. The new creatures of God must not be afraid of battle because of their number or limitations.

Where you need the strength of an army and yet you are alone, God can give you as an individual the strength of many people. In *Judges 15:15-16* God gave Samson the strength of an army and he single-handedly killed thousands of people. God is still giving the strength of an army to individuals who hope not in number but in Him. He can strengthen you to do what thousands of people cannot do. One with God is majority. The new creatures of God must declare in all situations that 'those who are with us are more than those who are with them (*2 Kings 6:16*).

8. PERSONAL ATTRIBUTES

There are those that put their hope in personal attributes. These could include beauty, physical strength, mental ability, intelligence, eloquence, family background, education, etc. Some people even boast of their citizenship. These are the thought of unregenerated man. In *Acts 12:21-23*, King Herod died violently because he put his trust in his personal attributes. *"And upon a set day Herod, arrayed in royal apparel, sat upon his throne, and made an oration unto them. And the people gave a shout, saying, 'It is the voice of a god, and not of a man'. And immediately the angel of the Lord smote him, because he gave not God the glory: and he was eaten of worms, and gave up the ghost."*

His personal attributes could not save him when heaven came against him. There are so many Herods around today and there are so many sons and daughters of Herod in our world. Their tongue is their pride. Their beauty is their hope. They talk and boast of things which are ephemeral. But very soon they will be stripped of their attributes and become naked. Moses disqualified himself for divine assignment in Exodus 4:10 because he thought it was all about eloquence. God proved him wrong. He used him without giving him a miracle of change of tongue to teach him a lesson that it is not all about physical attributes.

God is still using people for greater work with their disabilities. He performs miracles through them but still retains in their lives their physical limitations. This is to prove wrong those who put their hope and confidence in physical attributes. Hannah stated in *1 Samuel 2:9* that no man shall prevail by strength. This is the thought of a new creature of God. In *Philippians 3:4-8*, Paul, after he had gained the knowledge of a new creature, considered rubbish all his boasting about his attributes. He discovered that the knowledge of God is superior to the knowledge of the world. He discovered that it is better to be proud of being born of God than being born of man. He discovered that it is better to be proud of heavenly citizenship than the earthly one.

Are you a new creature? What is your boast? May God anoint you with the spirit of revelation and wisdom in Jesus' name.

Our New Hope

As new creatures the source of our hope and confidence has changed. It is written in *Hebrews 7:19* that the gospel of Jesus has brought to us a better hope. Our mind has been reprogrammed to function in a different manner. The new creatures have been translated into the kingdom of God. Now, the sources of our hope are:

A. GOD

Our salvation comes from God and so our hope is in Him.

> **1 Peter 1:21**
> Who by him do believe in God, that raised him up from the dead, and gave him glory; that your faith and hope might be in God.

The above states that God is our new hope. Hope put in God is a blessed hope. It can never fail. If your hope of success is because God will make it happen, you are blessed. When men failed Job during his darkest days, he put his hope in God.

> **Job 19:25**
> For I know that my redeemer liveth, and that he shall stand at the latter day upon the earth.

Job had strong confidence in the Almighty God. He saw Him as the ever-living redeemer. He put his total confidence in Him for restoration. He rejoiced in the hope of the glory of God and he was not disappointed. Hope in God never disappoints. It is written in *Habakkuk 2:3* that though the promise of God tarries, wait for it. This is because God is reliable and will never change. He is not limited in power, resources, space or influence.

He has all that you need in abundance. He will never cease to be God because He was not appointed by anybody neither was He voted into power. This gives assurance that He will always be available to attend to your demand. He cannot be manipulated against you because no man can bribe Him. He is always holy. The new creatures of God put their full confidence in God. He is the only one that can be with you in every situation as He stated in ***Isaiah 43:2***: *'When thou passest through the waters, I will be with thee; and through the rivers, they shall not overflow thee: when thou walkest through the fire, thou shalt not be burned; neither shall the flame kindle upon thee.'*

That is God for you, always with His children in all situations. He was with the three Hebrews when they were thrown inside fiery furnace (***Daniel 3:22-25***) and he was with the Israelites when they were passing through waters (***Exodus 14:29***).May God's presence never depart from your life in Jesus name.

B. GOD'S MERCY

One of the outstanding attributes of God is His mercy. His mercy stands out. The new creatures of God shall put their hope in God's mercy. We need His mercy to make us qualify for what we are not qualified for. There are victories that we are not qualified to get. There are positions that we are not qualified for. We don't always get it right but His mercy always prevails over judgement.

> **Psalms 33: 18**
> Behold, the eye of the LORD is upon them that fear him, upon them that hope in his mercy.

God never ignores the cry for His mercy. Exodus 34:6 affirms that God is merciful. Through His mercy, people that should have died have received another chance to live. God has allowed His mercy to make Him give food to those who do not deserve it. He has clothed the undeserving several times. By His mercy, he has set free those that should have died in captivity.

In **2 Samuel 24:14**, David chose to fall into the hand of God because he hoped in His mercy. David knew that God judges with mercy. If you also can put your hope in God's mercy, you will see yourself having access to blessings you don't deserve and victory that is beyond your ability. The mercy of God positions the weak for victory. May God's mercy position you for victory you don't deserve.

May God's mercy deliver you from every attack you have ignorantly invited into your life, In **Matthew 15:32-39**, Jesus had compassion on the crowd. He saw their situation and His heart was touched. Our God is a God that pities His children. He has sympathy. He cannot ignore the difficulty facing His children. Jesus fed the crowd with abundant food despite the fact that the crowd did not ask for food, though, they were hungry. Their situation communicated to Jesus that they needed help and the compassion in Jesus detected the signal. Even in your darkest hour, when all things fail, be assured that your God is watching and He will arise to show you mercy.

When you have ignorantly invited problem into your life don't lose hope because our God is a God that pities his children. He derives no satisfaction in seeing you wallowing in problems. His heart will be touched and he will arise for your sake. God knows that you are vulnerable and He understands that you won't always get it right so

He has made provision for mercy to deliver you from your difficult situations.

> **Hebrews 4:16**
> Let us therefore come boldly to the throne of grace, that we may obtain mercy and find grace to help in time of need.

When the enemy mocks you that you will never come out of the problem you have brought yourself into, put your hope in God's mercy. When you are too weak to cry for help, put your hope in God's mercy. When the enemy attacks your mind with guilt, put your hope in God's mercy. The mercy of God has no boundary and it is enduring. May God disappoint your mockers in Jesus name. May God prove your enemy wrong for your sake in Jesus name.

C. JESUS CHRIST

Jesus is the mediator of a new covenant according to *Hebrews 12:24*. He is a suitable intercessor. He mediates between man and God.

> **Hebrews 2:17-18**
> Wherefore in all things it behoved him to be made like unto his brethren, that he might be a merciful and faithful high priest in things pertaining to God, to make reconciliation for the sins of the people. For in that he himself hath suffered being tempted, he is able to succour them that are tempted.

The above shows that Jesus can feel our pains. He is able to intercede for us as we cry 'Abba father' to God. *1 Timothy 1:1: 'Paul, an apostle of Jesus Christ by the commandment of God our Saviour, and Lord Jesus Christ, which is our hope.'*

Jesus Christ is our hope. We can put our confidence in Him that He will intercede before God for our deliverance and salvation because He has experienced pains and suffering while He was on earth. As a new creature you must know that Jesus is the only one that can understand your pains and deepest needs. When you are misunderstood, hope in Jesus who was misunderstood while on earth. When no one seems to care for your needs, hope in Jesus because he was deserted when He was on earth. When you are lied against, hope in Jesus because he was lied against while He was on earth. When you are rejected and lonely, hope in Jesus because he was rejected and was lonely while He was on earth.

The new creatures of God should put their hope in Jesus for intercession for them. May God shed His light on your heart in Jesus name. May you continually see the glory of God around you in Jesus name.

D. GOD'S WORD

There are different kinds of words. There is the word of man and there is that of God. Man can speak but due to his limited ability, he is not able to establish his word in every situation. There are uncontrollable circumstances that are able to frustrate the word of man. Those who are wise among men put their hope in the Word of God. The new creatures of God must put their hope in the Word of God, not of man. There are so many reasons why the new creatures should put their hope in the Word of God. These include the facts that:

1. The word of God has protective power

> **Proverbs 30:5**
> Every word of God is pure: he is a shield unto them that put their trust in him.

That is, the Word of God is a shield to those that put their hope in it. If your life or any of your possession is under threat, put your hope in the word of God. It is written in *Psalm 91:7-8*, that you will only see evil befalling the wicked but it shall not come near you. This proves that you have immunity against the evil that befalls the people of the world. Stand on that word and you will see the threat flee before you. The word of God forms spiritual cover over your life. This cover is strong and no evil can penetrate it. May the word of God create a spiritual cover over your life in Jesus'name.

2. The word of God has life

> **Hebrews 4:12**
> For the word of God is quick, and powerful, and sharper than any two-edged sword, piercing even to the dividing asunder of soul and spirit, and of the joints and marrow, and is a discerner of the thoughts and intents of the heart.

The Word of God has life, so He is able to impart life even into a dead thing. If you release the word of God into your dead business, career or marriage, soon, it will come alive. The new creatures would put their hope of resurrection of their dead blessings in the word of God. In *2 Timothy 1:10*, it is stated that Jesus Christ has abolished death. As a new creature you can stand on this word of God and command every spirit of death to come out of your dead situation. Death has no power over any area of your life because Jesus has conquered death. Soon you will see your dead blessings come alive. I decree concerning your life today: no more death in Jesus name.

3. The Word of God grows

The Word of God can grow because it has life. The Word of God can enlarge in size. *Acts 19:20* says *'So mightily grew the word of God and prevailed.'* Wherever it is planted, situations change as it grows in size. Is your business sluggish or retarded? Release the Word of God into it. When you plant the Word of God in your business, soon you will see it growing as the Word of God planted inside of it grows. *Psalm 1:3* declares that whatever the righteous does prospers. Stand upon this Word of God and command your sluggish business and retarded career to flourish in Jesus name. Soon you will see growth in your life. The new creature should put their hope of growth in the Word of God. Your season to flourish has come in Jesus name.

4. The Word of God can travel

Locomotion is one of the attributes of living things.

Psalms 107:20
He sent his word, and healed them, and delivered them from their destructions.

The Word of God can travel from one location to another. It is not limited to a location. You can send the Word of God to do a job for you in a far place. In *John 4:52-53*, the son of a nobleman was healed at the same hour that Jesus released the Word. The Word travelled to locate the child where he was at that time. You can stay in the confines of your room and send the word of God to cause a change for you in a far place. I pray that as you decree a thing so shall it be established unto you in Jesus name.

5. The Word of God is mighty in its influence

Jeremiah 23:29
Is not my word like as a fire? saith the LORD; and like a hammer that breaketh the rock in pieces?

The new creatures put their hope in the Word of God because they know that there is no mountain it cannot remove. The Word of God is able to perform any operation it is employed to do. If you sent the Word of God to the Pharaoh of your life, he would be no more. Send the Word of God to that sickness and it will dissolve it. With the Word of God in action, that Herod of your life that is chasing you will be removed. **Isaiah 54:17** also gives the assurance that: *'No weapon that is formed against thee shall prosper; and every tongue that shall rise against thee in judgment thou shalt condemn. This is the heritage of the servants of the LORD, and their righteousness is of me, saith the LORD.'*

Stand on that Word of God and command failure upon every weapon the enemy fashions against your life and you will be amazed how fast it is destroyed. Only the Word of God can achieve such success. Put your hope in the Word of God and you will be a wonder to the world.

6. The Word of God is sweet and it can sweeten anything

> **Psalms 119:103**
> How sweet are thy words unto my taste! yea, sweeter than honey to my mouth!'

God's Word has ability to banish bitterness from a place. If your heart is bitter, invite the Word of God into it. If your life situation is bitter, send the word of God into it. If there is no motivation in your heart towards a good course, invite the word of God into your heart. Are you forsaken by a loved one? There is a hope in *Psalms 27:10* which states that: *'When my father and my mother forsake me, then the LORD will take me up.'*

Encourage yourself in the fact that you have a God that will never forsake you. God of the new creatures is abundantly able to take care of His own. Are men fashioning evil work against you? Be encouraged in the word.

> **2 Timothy 4:18**
> And the Lord shall deliver me from every evil work, and will preserve me unto his heavenly kingdom: to whom be glory for ever and ever.

Assure yourself of divine deliverance. Motivate yourself that your God will arise for your salvation. This will sweeten your heart. Are you in a great difficulty? *Romans 8:28* gives the assurance: *'And we know that all things work together for good to them that love God, to them who are the called according to his purpose.'*

Motivate yourself that God will cause all things to work for your good. Replace bad news with a good one and gladden your heart. Are you concerned that things may not go well in certain areas of your life? The word of God in **Isaiah 3:10** encourages us thus: *'Say ye to the righteous, that it shall be well with him: for they shall eat the fruit of their doings.'*

Tell yourself that it is well with you in Jesus name. Sweeten your heart with the Word of hope and your bones will receive strength. Are men telling you that your God has abandoned you? Take solace in **Job 19:25**, *'for I know that my redeemer liveth, and that he shall stand at the latter day upon the earth'*.

Tell yourself that your Redeemer lives and that he will arise for your sake. In the word of God, there is hope for the hopeless and strength for the weak. The new creatures of God should put their hope in the word of God. They should not hope in the words of men neither shall they hope in their own words. May God sweeten your life with His Word. May God remove every seed of bitterness and hopelessness from your life in Jesus'name.

7. The Word of God can never fail

The Word of God can never fail because the One who sends it has to defend His integrity. *Isaiah 55:11* shows the confidence of God's word: *'So shall my word be that goeth forth out of my mouth: it shall not return unto me void, but it shall accomplish that which I please, and it shall prosper in the thing whereto I sent it.*

In what way has the Word of God come to you? Is it as a word of instruction? If you obey it, you will prosper. Is it as a promise? It will come to pass. In *Matthew 24:35,* Jesus promised that His word would never go void. The promises of God shall come to pass. Hope in the Word of God and you will see a turn-around in your situation. The Lord that calls you is faithful - *1 Thessalonians 5:24.*

3

OUR YOKE HAS CHANGED

MATTHEW 11:28-30 invites: *'Come unto me, all ye that labour and are heavy laden, and I will give you rest. Take my yoke upon you, and learn of me; for I am meek and lowly in heart: and ye shall find rest unto your souls. For my yoke is easy, and my burden is light.'* The above shows that a born-again child of God has been delivered from the old yoke(handed over to him from the world) to the new yoke(handed over to him by Jesus Christ).

What is a yoke?

A yoke is a wooden beam used between a pair of oxen to allow them to pull a load. There is a yoke driver that ensures that the animals drive the load on a preferred path. Spiritually, a yoke is anything that compels a person to function in a certain way against his will. The person under a yoke is subjected to situation he can't control. A yoke does not permit free movement. The yoke driver dictates everything. Prior to regeneration, there were so many situations that a person could be subjected to, that serve as yokes. These are old yokes. Examples of such old yokes are:

1. YOKE OF SELF-RIGHTEOUSNESS

In the old life, we counted righteousness through what we did externally, so we worked hard to achieve it in our own way. We wanted to make ourselves good. Man established his own righteousness. **Romans 10:3:** *'For they being ignorant of God's righteousness, and going about to establish their own righteousness, have not submitted themselves unto the righteousness of God.'*

Due to ignorance, man went to establish his own righteousness through series of laws to enable him to be righteous, according to **Romans 3:20**. He labours a lot and lives in the bondage he put himself, in an attempt to observe all the rules and regulation he has set for himself. He also lives a life of regret whenever he violates any of the set rules. In **Luke 18:12**, a Pharisee was boasting of his righteousness based on his personal efforts. To him, it is all about personal effort, not the grace of God.

> **Job 14:4**
> Who can bring a clean thing out of an unclean? not one.

No man can make an unclean thing clean without God. You will never be able to make yourself perfect; neither will you be able to make yourself good. The reason why you hate yourself whenever you make a mistake is because you want to make yourself righteous. The life of the spirit cannot be achieved through human effort and any attempt to do so will lead to a yoke.

Acts 1:8 gives the key: *'But ye shall receive power, after that the Holy Ghost is come upon you: and ye shall be witnesses unto* *me both in Jerusalem, and in all Judea, and in Samaria, and unto the uttermost part of the earth.'*

The power of the Holy Spirit is to enable you to live a righteous life with ease. If you have to struggle to live a holy life, it means you need more assistance from the Holy Spirit, not from your flesh.

2 Corinthians 5:21 says *'For he hath made him to be sin for us, who knew no sin; that we might be made the righteousness of God in him'.*

A new creature of God has already attained righteousness in God and he does not need any effort to be righteous. You have been made clean and as long as you walk in obedience to God's Word, the blessings of God will continually flow into your life. You don't need another set of rules or another guide. What God has provided in His kingdom is enough. Don't yoke yourself with any human regulations and tradition. Don't let the enemy deceive you to live a life of the Spirit with human effort. It is a frustrating thing to do.

2. YOKE OF GUILT

In the old life there was no provision for dealing with guilt, so we carried it through life until we met Jesus. When a wrong thing is done, it leaves behind the stain of guilt. Unless the person comes under the cleansing blood of Jesus, he will carry this yoke through life. We learn from Genesis 50:15-20 thus *'And when Joseph's brethren saw that their father was dead, they said, Joseph will peradventure hate us, and will certainly requite us all the evil which we did unto him. And they sent a messenger unto Joseph, saying, Thy father did command before he died, saying, so shall ye say unto Joseph, Forgive, I pray thee now, the trespass of thy brethren, and their sin; for they did unto thee evil: and now, we pray thee, forgive the trespass of the servants of the God of thy father. And Joseph wept when they spake unto him. And his brethren also went and fell down before his face; and they said, Behold, we be thy servants. And Joseph said unto them, Fear not: for am I in the place of God? But as for you, ye thought evil against me; but God meant it unto good, to bring to pass, as it is this day, to save much people alive.'* The above story shows the strength of guilt. Many years after the brothers of Joseph had sold him into slavery, they still carried the guilt. Despite all the provisions and acceptance they received from Joseph they still carried the guilt. This is an example of a yoke. This shows that you can be forgiven but if you refuse to forgive yourself, it brings guilt. The world has no provision for dealing with guilt outside the kingdom of God. Guilt takes away joy and it brings condemnation. If it is not dealt with, it can lead to self-hatred and suicide. Furthermore, **2 Corinthians 7:10** says *'for godly sorrow worketh repentance to salvation not to be repented of: but the sorrow of the world worketh death.'*

The above shows that if guilt is not dealt with, using the provision in God's kingdom, it may lead to death. In **Matthew 27:3**, Judas killed himself due to guilt. We get our boldness from **Hebrews 4:16** which encourages us thus: *'Let us therefore come boldly unto the throne of grace, that we may obtain mercy, and find grace to help in time of need.'*

That is, there is provision for mercy, to help us to deal with guilt instead of carrying it through life.

> **1 John 1:9**
> If we confess our sins, he is faithful and just to forgive us our sins, and to cleanse us from all unrighteousness.

This is the guarantee that after confession has been made concerning the wrong done, we should move on with our lives with an assurance that we have been made clean and forgiven. No more guilt. No more regret over anything. Live as if nothing of such has ever happened to you.

3. YOKE OF FALSE TEACHING

1 Timothy 4:1 says *'Now the Spirit speaketh expressly, that in the latter times some shall depart from the faith, giving heed to seducing spirits, and doctrines of devils.'* False teachings come through the devil to rob man of his freedom in Jesus. These doctrines are designed by the enemy to lead people away from God and yoke them with demonic instructions. They make man to accept bondage with good reasons that have their origin in demonic manipulation. They come with series of rules that appear reasonable but they are ungodly. Every doctrine that contradicts the Holy Bible is demonic and if followed, they take away the liberty that Jesus gave to his followers.

> **Colossians 2:20-21**
> Wherefore if ye be dead with Christ from the rudiments of the world, why, as though living in the world, are ye subject to ordinances, (touch not; taste not; handle not...)

False teachings come in different forms such as in things to touch, things not to or otherwise. They could be regulations about whom to marry or not. They are all about what to do or not to do; but not about what God says concerning every situation. The motive was to take liberty away from man. In the old life before regeneration, we followed all these doctrines that made our lives miserable and difficult. As new creatures, we no longer live under such bondage. It is time for you to enjoy fully all the freedom God has given you through Jesus Christ and don't yoke yourself with series of doctrines that have their root in the pit of hell. Don't allow demons to dictate to you what you should eat or drink. Don't let demons lure you into devil worship through false freedom that in reality is bondage. Say no to teachings that glorify sins. Don't follow instructions that contradict the Bible. Whatever you can't see in the Bible is not permitted by God, irrespective of who said it. For other foundation can no man lay than that is laid, which is Jesus Christ (**1 Corinthians 3:11**).

4. YOKE OF TRADITION

> **Matthew 15:6**
> And honour not his father or his mother, he shall be free. Thus have ye made the commandment of God of none effect by your tradition.

Tradition fuels dogma that sets aside God's commands. Following human tradition robs a man the full enjoyment of the blessings of salvation. Tradition is a pollutant designed to adulterate the truth. Perhaps before you became a Christian you used to observe the traditions of your family and participate in family festivals. Have you ever questioned the origin of such festivals? You will be amazed to know that it probably originated from demonic channels. Tradition can be a yoke which will not let you experience the power of the Holy Spirit, because it is impossible for light and darkness to co-exist. Observing family traditions will hinder the effectiveness of the power of the gospel of Jesus Christ in your life. A new creature of God should observe only the laws of Jesus Christ.

Matthew 6:24 says *'No man can serve two masters: for either he will hate the one, and love the other; or else he will hold to the one, and despise the other. Ye cannot serve God and mammon.'*

You can't observe two traditions without falling into accusation. A new creature of God observes only the tradition of God. The old tradition you received through parental lineage must be totally replaced with that of God, otherwise you will not experience the flow of the power of God in your life and it will make the gospel of Jesus to be of no effect in your situations.

5. YOKE OF AMBITION

God wants His children to have goals and visions but He wants to be the origin of it all. Ambition is an earnest desire for an achievement and the willingness to strive for its attainment. It becomes a yoke if it takes away freedom and causes anxiety. Its origin will determine how it will be pursued and attained. In the old life there was a way we pursued goals that invited yokes. There is an example in *1 Kings 21:1-4:* *'And it came to pass after these things, that Naboth the Jezreelite had a vineyard, which was in Jezreel, hard by the palace of Ahab king of Samaria. And Ahab spake unto*

Naboth, saying, Give me thy vineyard, that I may have it for a garden of herbs, because it is near unto my house: and I will give thee for it a better vineyard than it; or, if it seem good to thee, I will give thee the worth of it in money. And Naboth said to Ahab, The LORD forbid it me, that I should give the inheritance of my fathers unto thee. And Ahab came into his house heavy and displeased because of the word which Naboth the Jezreelite had spoken to him: for he had said, I will not give thee the inheritance of my fathers. And he laid him down upon his bed, and turned away his face, and would eat no bread.'

King Ahab could not sleep because his ambition has put a yoke on him. A goal that makes you sleepless and takes away your comfort has become a yoke. God's vision does not bring a yoke because since it originated from Him it shall be established by Him. The new creature of God should always have peace, irrespective of the situation around him. When God gives a vision, he also gives provision. God will not give you a vision that will take away your peace. May God's grace be abundant upon you to dwell in peace always in Jesus' Name.

6. YOKE OF FEAR

Whatever you are afraid of apart from God is a yoke. Fear takes away liberty. It compels people to function in certain ways that are against their will. Fear gives a person the wrong identity. In **Genesis 12:10-14**, Abram and Sara lied that they were not husband and wife due to fear. They did not lie because they were liars but because they were afraid of what the Egyptians would do to them if they revealed their true identities. In the old life, due to lack of a relationship with God, we devised many ways of escape from certain challenging situations. As a new creature of God, you now have God who is always available to defend and protect you in every situation. You can now damn any consequence of telling the truth always because you have God on your side. Our God is able to handle any difficulty that telling the truth could invite into our lives. You can no longer allow fear to dictate to you how to handle challenges and difficult situations. You can no longer allow fear of what may happen to enslave and drive you around. Tell the truth to shame the devil, and let your God handle the aftermath.

Our New Yoke

Matthew 11:28-30 which we cited earlier invites us to: *'Come unto me, all ye that labour and are heavy laden, and I will give you rest. Take my yoke upon you, and learn of me; for I am meek and lowly in heart: and ye shall find rest unto your souls. For my yoke is easy, and my burden is light.'*

Jesus has a yoke. What is his yoke? The answer is in *1 John 5:3:* *'For this is the love of God, that we keep his commandments: and his commandments are not grievous.'* God's commandments are the yokes of Jesus. As a new creature of God the only yoke you should carry around is the yoke of Jesus. Obedience without compromise. If you can take this yoke, you will be free from every other yokes in the world today. Those who obey God will be feared by the world and not the other way round. Such people will be free from every doctrine of man. They will also have no need of following other rules that cause bondage. They will be free from common problems of the world such as anxiety, fear, sickness, hardship and the likes.

What makes the yoke of Jesus easy?

Deuteronomy 30:11-14 tells us: *'For this commandment which I command thee this day, it is not hidden from thee, neither is it far off. It is not in heaven, that thou shouldest say, Who shall go up for us to heaven, and bring it unto us, that we may hear it, and do it? Neither is it beyond the sea, that thou shouldest say, Who shall go over the sea for us, and bring it unto us, that we may hear it, and do it? But the word is very nigh unto thee, in thy mouth, and in thy heart, that thou mayest do it.'*

The above shows that our God is not complicated in his dealing with us. His rules are not strange. God will not ask you to do what you are not capable of doing. He makes a demand according to your ability. It is the people of the world that will demand from you what you can't offer. The devil will always ask from you what will put you into debt and serious trouble. As a new creature you must have delight in obeying God. His spirit dwells in you to give you the grace. May God make you His true worshipper in Jesus Name. May He give you more grace to function as a new creature.

4

OUR FEAR HAS CHANGED

THERE ARE TWO TYPES of fear: Godly and ungodly fear. The godly fear is a reverential fear we show to our God. It is godly fear that makes us to relate with God with respect and honour without disobedience. The ungodly fear is a painful emotion that originates from expectation of evil or danger. It comes with anxiety and leads to bondage.

A. Ungodly Fear - the Old Fear

In the old life, we lived under ungodly fear because there was no relationship with God. Examples of things we used to fear include:

1. FEAR OF MEN

This made us to be men pleasers because we didn't want to offend men. Many people prefer to disobey God in order to please men. *1 Samuel 15:24* gives an example: *'And Saul said unto Samuel, I have sinned: for I have transgressed the commandment of the Lord, and thy words: because I feared the people, and obeyed their voice.'* Saul disobeyed God because he feared the people. He decided to sway unto the side of men when there was contradiction between God's demand

and that of men. Saul lost his position that God gave him. The fear of men will make you lose the blessings you have received from God. If you have a record of losing things such as opportunities, it may be due to fear of men. Whatever you are afraid of will oppress your life. The fear of men will make you treat people differentially and this will raise attackers against you.

2. FEAR OF THE UNKNOWN

This generates insecurity. If it takes root in your life, it drives you to make series of ungodly effort to secure your future. You can practice covetousness in the attempt to secure your future.

Matthew 6:25 says *'Therefore I say unto you, Take no thought for your life, what ye shall eat, or what ye shall drink; nor yet for your body, what ye shall put on. Is not the life more than meat, and the body than raiment?'* Jesus told his disciples not to be anxious about the future as God is in control of it. Jesus instructed his disciples not to take anything along when sending them out in *Luke 9:3* and it was confirmed that though they went out with nothing, yet they lacked nothing (*Luke 22:35*). In the old life, our future was in our hands because we had no relationship with God who owns the future.

3. FEAR OF DANGER

A man who has no relationship with God will be anxious when he faces danger. In the old life, we lived under the fear of danger. In *Matthew 14:30,* instead of rebuking the wind, the disciples cried when faced with the storm. Unregenerated people cannot tame the devil because they have no power of the Spirit to do so. In *2 King 6:15*, the servant of Elisha cried out when he saw enemies advancing toward himself and his master. He was afraid because he could not feel the presence of God around him. In the old life, we lived under fear because there was no presence of God around us. We were very vulnerable. There was no weapon of warfare.

4. FEAR OF CONDEMNATION

This is a fear that arises when a fault is committed. You hide or lie when an error is committed because of the fear of being rebuked or condemned. There is no boldness to tell the truth and apologise for the error committed in order to shame the devil. This is evil. In *Genesis 3:8*, we see an example: *'And they heard the voice of the LORD God walking in the garden in the cool of the day: and Adam and his wife hid themselves from the presence of the LORD God amongst the trees of the garden.'* In the old life, we preferred to hide instead of apologising for our error. We were too afraid of condemnation. We did not have the knowledge of God's love because there was no relationship with Him. We did not even know that God judges with love.

5. FEAR OF FAILURE

This is the fear that makes a man not to try new things because he is afraid of failure. If you have failed in certain things when you attempt to try it again the devil will remind you of your past failure and this would put fear in you. You stop trying again because you don't want to fail again. In the old life the possibility of failure was more real than that of success. It is because we managed our own life affairs.

6. FEAR OF BATTLE AGAINST STRONGER ENEMIES

This manifests through acceptance of defeat even before the battle begins. You surrender and accept defeat because you believe you can't withstand your enemies. In Deuteronomy 20:1, God told the Israelites not to be afraid of enemies that appear stronger than them because the battle will be fought by their God, not themselves.

7. FEAR OF EXPOSURE OF SECRETS

This manifests through eye-service or unnecessary and excessive respect for a person who knows your secret. You turn the person into an idol because you are afraid of him or her exposing your secret. The best way to handle such fear is to expose the secret yourself. Let the people you don't want to know about the secret know about it through you. Prayerfully expose the secret to them and your God will handle the rest. Don't turn yourself into a slave because somebody knows your secret. You are a new creature; you can no longer live under fear.

8. FEAR OF OTHER GODS

This manifests through forming alliances with other gods as a way of appeasing them. You decide to reconcile with witches and wicked people because you are afraid of their power. In *2 Kings 17:35-38,* it is stated that God warned the Israelites not to be afraid of other gods and never to form any alliance with them. In reality, the devil can never love anyone, whether you form an alliance with him or not. Even those who served the devil received the wages of sorrow and death. When Judas worked for the devil by selling out Jesus, the devil paid him with suicide. He will be in hell with the devil for eternity. As long as you remain in the Lord, no evil power can dominate or harm you.

9. FEAR OF DEATH

The fear of death hinders people from taking any risk. Such people can't conquer new territories because of the fear of death. They live in bondage and never make exploits. ***Hebrews 2:15*** declares that some people live under bondage throughout their lifetime due to the fear of death. History has shown that those who fear death never live long. The fear of death kills them prematurely.

10. NEEDLESS OR UNEXPLAINABLE FEAR

This manifest in an individual being unable to explain what is making them to be afraid. Fear comes in for no credible or tenable reason. ***Psalm 53:5*** says that some people are in great fear where no fear was. It is because fear is a spirit and once it is allowed, it makes its victim to be irrational. There are numerous manifestations of this tormenting, binding, ensnaring fear apparent in our world today. Multitudes of people fear for their safety, hiding behind closed doors and barred windows, arming themselves with lethal weapons. People also fear rejection, pain, sickness, poverty, and even old age.

Other Types of Fear

There are so many other types of fear that psychologists have discovered. Examples of such fears described as common "phobias" include the following:

Acrophobia: The fear of height

Agoraphobia: Fear of open and public places

Achmophobia: The fear of sharp objects

Algophobia: Fear of pain

Anthropophobia: Fear of man or a particular person

Astraphobia: Fear of thunder, lightning, or storms

Claustrophobia: A fear of closed places

Ereuthophobia: Fear of blushing

Gynephobia: Fear of women or a particular woman

Hematophobia: Fear of blood

Hydrophobia: Fear of water

Monophobia: Fear of solitude

Necrophobia: Fear of dead bodies

Nyctophobia: Fear of darkness

Ochlophobia: Fear of crowds

Pathophobia: Fear of disease

Pyrophobia: Fear of fire

Thanatophobia: Fear of death

Toxiphobia: Fear of poisons

Zoophobia: Fear of animals

Note: Living under any of the above types of fear is a sin. They need to be confronted and overcome. As a new creature, you can no longer allow fear to rule over you.

Confronting Your Fear

> **Job 3:25**
> For the things I greatly feared has come upon me and what I dreaded has happened to me.

That is, whatever you are afraid of will eventually happen to you. Fear is a spirit and operates through the circumstances of life. The devil takes advantage of life situations to send the spirit of fear to us so that we lose the freedom God has given us through Jesus Christ.

For example, if you have the history of failure in a particular area of your life, when you attempt to try again, the devil will remind you of your last failure and make you afraid of trying again. He will make you afraid of failure and since it has happened before, you are likely to fall into that deception by believing him. This may stop you from trying again.

Until you rise against what is making you afraid, you will never come out of its dominion because whatever makes you afraid, if you don't rise against it, will continue to suppress and oppress you.

Similarly, whatever makes you afraid will control the entirety of your life - your thoughts, words, actions, expectation, imaginations, plans and dreams. These will bring into manifestation what you are afraid of. If care is not taken whatever you are afraid of will befall you. You need to eliminate whatever fear you have for many reasons. It is important that you do away with your fear quickly because:

WHATEVER YOU ARE AFRAID OF WILL LIKELY BEFALL YOU.

There are numerous examples of this in the Bible.

a. In *Numbers 13 and 14*, the Israelites were afraid of death due to the fear of the Amalekites and they started confessing death and eventually died.

b. In *1 Samuel 15:24-26*, King Saul was afraid of losing his throne so he preferred to obey the people instead of God, eventually he lost the throne.

c. In *2 Chronicles 16:9*, King Asa was afraid of war and sought help from unbelievers instead of God. He eventually had wars and died.

d. In *Haggai 1:4-10*, the Israelites were afraid of poverty so they did not pay their tithes or build the house of God. They remained poor and were never able to build their own houses.

WHATEVER YOU ARE AFRAID OF WILL FOLLOW YOU AROUND.

In *1 Kings 19:1- 4* Elijah was afraid of death in the hands of Jezebel and later became suicidal in his thoughts. He ran away from death but still expected death. What a contradiction! Elijah developed the thought of death due to fear and the thought of death followed him around.

WHATEVER YOU ARE AFRAID OF WILL EXPAND ITS TERRITORY IN YOUR LIFE.

Ben-hadad, in *I Kings 20: 5-6*, demanded the wife and children of King Ahab who consented to the demand. Because of this, Ben-hadad went further and demanded the entire throne of King Ahab who now discovered that he was in a serious problem. Fear expands its territory when it is allowed to operate without check. If you fear your manager at work, soon, you will begin to fear the deputy manager and later the assistant deputy manager, then the secretary and eventually, all your colleagues. If you still fail to confront your fear, it will continue to rule over you until it reduces you to nothing. Many under the yoke of fear lose their self-esteem.

Unless you confront your fear, it will never go. In *1 Samuel 17*, David rose against Goliath whom everybody was afraid of and he overcame him in battle. In *1 Chronicles 4:10*, Jabez rose against the curse his mother placed upon him and overcame it in prayer. He decided to confront it instead of remaining under self-pity and fear of laying hand on good things due to imminent failure. In the book of Exodus, Moses confronted King Pharaoh relentlessly and got the Israelites free from bondage. He did not stop until his enemy surrendered.

In *Daniel 3:17-27*, the three Hebrews confronted the fire the enemy had put in place and subdued it. They refused to bow down to the fire or stay under the fear of it. In *Nehemiah 4:13-16*, Nehemiah confronted the enemies of his calling and he saw their end. He refused to live under fear. He refused to surrender his vision.

How Can You Confront Your Fear?

1. CONFRONT YOUR FEAR IN GOD'S NAME

David confronted Goliath in God's name. *'Then said David to the Philistine, Thou comest to me with a sword, and with a spear, and with a shield: but I come to thee in the name of the LORD of hosts, the God of the armies of Israel, whom thou hast defied.'*(**1 Samuel 17:45**). The reason you are afraid of that situation or that person is because you consider the situation or the person greater than you; so remove your name and replace it with the name of God.

> **Deuteronomy 20:1**
> When thou goest out to battle against thine enemies, and seest horses, and chariots, and a people more than thou, be not afraid of them: for the LORD thy God is with thee, which brought thee up out of the land of Egypt.

That is, when battles come, it is the God of the Israelites that is facing the battle, not the Israelites. **1 John 4:4** emphasises that *'Greater is he that is in you than he that is in the world.'*

Make God your focus, not yourself or your ability. If there is any fear at your workplace, when you go to work tell yourself 'God has come to work, not me'. In that instance, you don't arrive at work under the fear of your boss or of how to do the work. It is not about you, but your God.

When you go for an interview, tell yourself that God has come for the interview, not you. Consequently you won't face the interview in fear. When you are being challenged by anybody, tell yourself that God is being challenged, not you.

When a word of failure is directed at you, tell yourself that the word is directed at God, not you. When you are threatened by any situation, tell yourself God is being threatened, not you.

Stop making yourself the victim; push it over to God who has unlimited ability.

2. CONFRONT YOUR FEAR WITH PASSION

> **1 Samuel 17:48**
> And it came to pass, when the Philistine arose, and came and drew nigh to meet David, that David hasted, and ran toward the army to meet the Philistine.

David ran into battle against Goliath. He was so excited to face Goliath; he did not face Goliath crying. You don't face your fears by begging or weeping but by being active when confronting them. The enemy will be watching your body-language to detect if your show of boldness is real or if you are just pretending. So, if you are going to demand your right from your oppressive manager, you have to show passion, boldness and be active. If you are shy and lack confidence, looking downwards, he or she will not take you serious. Lift up your head and confront situations boldly!

3. CONFRONT YOUR FEAR BY DISREGARDING THE THREAT

In confronting your fear, you have to shift your focus from the capability of your enemy and focus on the capability of your God. In *Daniel 3:18-19*, the three Hebrews disregarded the capability of fire to burn and focused on the capability of their God to save. Even when the king commanded that the power of the fire should be increased seven times, the three Hebrews were not moved. They remained focused on the capability of their God. If you are going to apply for a job, for example, you don't focus on the capability of what you don't have to disqualify you, but you focus on the capability of your God to back you up. There was a crippled lady who applied for a job in a secondary school. The panel gave her the job based on the fact that her disability limits her being able to effectively move around to search for a job. For the other able applicants, they could easily move around in their job search. God used her limitation to her advantage. May God use your limitation for your advantage in Jesus 'name.

4. CONFRONT YOUR FEAR RESOLUTELY

That is, no retreat no surrender. Make up your mind that you will not accept anything different from victory. When you decide to demand for freedom, don't stop until it is granted. Don't start what you will not finish. When King Pharaoh refused to let Israel go in *Exodus 5:1-10*, Moses kept on confronting him until the people gained their freedom. Never abandon the struggle for freedom. Why? It is because abandonment will increase the bondage. For example, once you have made up your mind to come out of sickness, ensure that you don't stop seeking for healing until you get it; otherwise, the pain of the sickness will increase. Note that the reason why fear increases when it is no longer being attacked is to make it difficult for you to demand for your freedom again. May God make you stronger than your enemy in Jesus'name.

5. CONFRONT YOUR FEAR WITH WATCHING AND PRAYING

Fear is a spirit so it needs spiritual attention. In *Nehemiah 4:9*, the people prayed and set a watch. When you decide to come out of fear, the enemy will try another game but if you watch as you pray, you will not fall into his trap. Many people, due to carelessness, enter into another problem as they emerge from one. When the enemies of Nehemiah discovered that they had failed in their attempt to use fear and mockery to stop the work, they tried blackmail but Nehemiah overcame; he did not fall for it. May God strengthen your hands in Jesus' name. As you rise against your fear, it will flee from you in Jesus name. Whatever is making you to be afraid shall surrender to you in Jesus name.

B. Godly Fear-the New Fear

Our fear has changed. What we fear has changed. We shall fear only God. To fear God is to reverence him in all your ways.

> **Hebrews 12:28**
> Wherefore we receiving a kingdom which cannot be moved, let us have grace, whereby we may serve God acceptably with reverence and godly fear.

As a new creature of God you should fear only God. The reason being that if you fear God, you will not need to fear any other thing again. Once you fear God, whatever the challenges you face will be dealt with directly by the God who you fear. Evidence of fear of God manifests through obedience to His word. You fear God when you obey all His commandments. You fear God when you hate what He hates and love what He loves. You fear God when you honour Him in all your ways.

> **Deuteronomy 10:12**
> And now, Israel, what doth the LORD thy God require of thee, but to fear the LORD thy God, to walk in all his ways, and to love him, and to serve the LORD thy God with all thy heart and with all thy soul.

You truly fear God when all your decisions are based on glorifying Him, not yourself.

Benefits of Fearing God

1.   IT MAKES YOU HOLY

The fear of God produces holiness in your lifestyle. A man who fears God will always be holy. You cannot fear God and still practice sins. *2 Corinthians 7:1* reads *'Having therefore these promises, dearly beloved, let us cleanse ourselves from all filthiness of the flesh and spirit, perfecting holiness in the fear of God.'*

2.   IT PRODUCES DIVINE WISDOM IN YOU

Proverbs 1:7 says *'The fear of the LORD is the beginning of knowledge: but fools despise wisdom and instruction.'* You can't fear God and still remain foolish. As a new creature of God who embraces the fear of God, His knowledge will always be with you.

3. IT QUALIFIES YOU FOR DIVINE ACCEPTANCE

Acts 10:35 says *'But in every nation he that feareth him, and worketh righteousness, is accepted with him.'* Nothing can make God reject whatever that is of you or from you when you fear Him. You will always be accepted in God eyes. Your sacrifice, labour of love and the services that you render in God's name will all be accepted by Him. Even the imagination of your heart and your desires will all be acceptable to God. What a blessing to fear God!

4. IT QUALIFIES YOU FOR DIVINE MERCY

Luke 1:50 says *'And his mercy is on them that fear him from generation to generation.'* As you demonstrate the fear of God in all your ways, you will always enjoy God's mercy.

Fear Not!

When you fear God, then fear cannot dominate or emanate from any area of your life because there is no void.

> **Matthew 10:28**
> And fear not them which kill the body, but are not able to kill the soul: but rather fear him which is able to destroy both soul and body in hell.

Why fear not? *Matthew 10:31* -*'Fear ye not therefore, ye are of more value than many sparrows.'* Jesus told his disciples to fear not. As a new creature, Jesus is telling you also to fear not. There are several reasons why you should not fear:

1. THERE WILL BE DIVINE PROVISIONS

1 Kings 17:13-14 says *'And Elijah said unto her, Fear not; go and do as thou hast said: but make me thereof a little cake first, and bring it unto me, and after make for thee and for thy son. For thus saith the LORD God of Israel, The barrel of meal shall not waste, neither shall the cruse of oil fail, until the day that the LORD sendeth rain upon the earth.'* In the midst of famine God remembered a poor widow. That God is still alive and He is still in the business of supplying the needs of those who have needs. Fear not, because God will supply all your needs according to His riches in glory.

2. THERE ARE BLESSINGS IN YOUR FUTURE

Something good is awaiting you in future, so, don't be afraid of the future.

> **Jeremiah 31:17**
> And there is hope in thine end, saith the LORD, that thy children shall come again to their own border.

As God has promised that there is hope in the future; there are blessings in your tomorrow. **Genesis 26:24** says *'And the LORD appeared unto him the same night, and said, I am the God of Abraham thy father: fear not, for I am with thee, and will bless thee, and multiply thy seed for my servant Abraham's sake.'* The God who holds the future had promised blessings in your tomorrow. Don't be afraid of your future because it shall be glorious.

3. GOD STRENGTHENS THE WEAK

God shall supply strength when you need it. So don't be afraid of your limitations.

> **Isaiah 41:10**
> Fear thou not; for I am with thee: be not dismayed; for I am thy God: I will strengthen thee; yea, I will help thee; yea, I will uphold thee with the right hand of my righteousness.

God is promising you that your weakness shall not limit you, because He will strengthen you. You can now say with boldness that: 'I can do all things through Christ that strengthen me.'

4. YOU SHALL NOT BE ALONE IN TRIAL

Don't be afraid of test because you will never be alone. God will always be with you in all your trials. *Isaiah 43:1-2* says *'But now thus saith the LORD that created thee, O Jacob, and he that formed thee, O Israel, Fear not: for I have redeemed thee, I have called thee by thy name; thou art mine. When thou passest through the waters, I will be with thee; and through the rivers, they shall not overflow thee: when thou walkest through the fire, thou shalt not be burned; neither shall the flame kindle upon thee.'* The Holy one of Israel is giving you a promise that He will always be with you in all your confrontation, so, don't be afraid of the test and trials of life. No challenge shall overpower you because the God that is greater than the greatest will always be with you.

5. THERE SHALL BE PROTECTION IN DANGER

Fear no evil because you will only see it and hear about it but it shall not come to you. God has provided adequate security for you in the journey of life.

Psalms 91:7-10 gives the assurance that *'A thousand shall fall at thy side, and ten thousand at thy right hand; but it shall not come nigh thee. Only with thine eyes shalt thou behold and see the reward of the wicked. Because thou hast made the LORD, which is my refuge, even the most High, thy habitation; there shall no evil befall thee, neither shall any plague come nigh thy dwelling.'*

God has provided divine immunity for you. You are immune against every evil of the world.

6. GOD CARES FOR YOU

You will not be afraid of your survival.

> **Matthew 10:30-31**
> But the very hairs of your head are all numbered. Fear ye not therefore, ye are of more value than many sparrows.'

The value of an article determines the level of its care from the owner. You are precious in the eye of the Lord so, He cares about your survival. God has made provision for your care; fear not. Due to your value, God is not ready to allow the enemy to mess you up. God needs you and that is why He created you.

7. YOU ARE STRONGER THAN THE GRAVE

Do not be afraid of death; it is not the end but the beginning of a better experience. Resist every attempt of the enemy to threaten you with death.

OUR **FEAR** HAS CHANGED

> **Revelation 1:17-18**
> And when I saw him, I fell at his feet as dead. And he laid his right hand upon me, saying unto me, Fear not; I am the first and the last: I am he that liveth, and was dead; and, behold, I am alive for evermore, Amen; and have the keys of hell and of death.'

The keys of hell and of death are in the hands of your God, not the devil. It is your God that will determine who should die and who should live. When the devil threatens you with the fear of death, resist him; you can't die until God wants you home. Take more risk, try new things, nothing can kill you until your time is up. Don't be stagnant because of the fear of death. Try new ideas. Fear not; you are a new creature.

5

OUR HEARTS HAVE CHANGED

THE HEART IS THE CENTRE of man's character – what he really is.

> **Luke 6:45**
> A good man out of the good treasure of his heart bringeth forth that which is good; and an evil man out of the evil treasure of his heart bringeth forth that which is evil: for of the abundance of the heart his mouth speaketh.

The above shows a set of two characters originating from two set of hearts. The two set of hearts could be described as the Evil heart and the Good heart. The evil heart is the heart of the unregenerated man(the old man)while the good heart is that of a regenerated man(the new man).We shall look into each of the two types of heart to enable a born-again man keep himself/herself under check and to avoid their hearts drifting or changing into the evil hearts.

The Evil Heart—the Old Man

Everyman has an evil heart unless he comes to Jesus for salvation of his soul. Until a man accepts Jesus as his personal Lord and Saviour, he has an evil heart.

Ezekiel 36:26-27 says 'A new heart also will I give you, and a new spirit will I put within you: and I will take away the stony heart out of your flesh, and I will give you an heart of flesh. And I will put my spirit within you, and cause you to walk in my statutes, and ye shall keep my judgments, and do them.' An evil heart is a stony heart. It is an un-renewed heart. It is a heart everyman is born with. There is no potential of doing God's will in an evil heart. It can never be made good or improved on unless it is completely replaced. The evil heart is so terrible that there is nothing that can be done to make it good. That is why God states in the above verse (***Ezekiel 36:26-27***) that the evil heart has to be replaced because it cannot be made good. Nothing can make a man good before God unless he accepts Jesus Christ and receive a fresh heart from God.

Characteristics of an Evil Heart

1. HARDENED IN NATURE

> **Exodus 4:21**
> And the LORD said unto Moses, When thou goest to return into Egypt, see that thou do all those wonders before Pharaoh, which I have put in thine hand: but I will harden his heart, that he shall not let the people go.

A man of an evil heart will refuse to obey God's most wise, just, and reasonable commands. He does not change his stand neither does he show flexibility on an issue, no matter how serious the consequences will be. Do you open yourself up for a change of decision if there is enough justification for it or do you stubbornly maintain your stand even when it is clear that you are wrong? If you answer 'No' you are still operating with a hardened heart.

2. FULL OF EVIL IMAGINATION

> **Genesis 6:5**
> And GOD saw that the wickedness of man was great in the earth, and that every imagination of the thoughts of his heart was only evil continually.

The evil heart imagines evil always. Its purposes and desires are evil. This kind of heart lacks the ability to generate good things. The spirit that works with it is evil so it produces evil. There is evil in our world today because the hearts of people are evil. They wish other people dead and desire that situations should go wrong in someone else's life. Do you plot evil and desire it? Do you imagine evil against somebody? If 'yes,' you need another heart.

3. SET TO DO EVIL

> **Ecclesiastes 8: 11**
> Because sentence against an evil work is not executed speedily, therefore the heart of the sons of men is fully set in them to do evil.

An evil heart justifies doing evil whenever it feels God is delaying judgement. It punishes its enemy in order to revenge. It considers God's mercy an indulgence to sinners, so it sets itself up to punish presumed sinner or its offenders. Only an evil heart seeks for revenge. Do you get angry when you see God showing mercy to your offender? If 'yes' you need another heart.

4. WICKED

> **Jeremiah 17:9**
> The heart is deceitful above all things, and desperately wicked: who can know it?

The evil heart is incurably wicked. It does not only practice wickedness, but it also rejoices in it. It derives its pleasure from wickedness. Everything that makes it happy is evil. The cry and sorrow of other people does not move it. A man of an evil heart is wicked and has no mercy for the weak. Does that describe you? It is time to repent.

5. FAR FROM GOD

> **Matthew 15:8**
> This people draweth nigh unto me with their mouth, and honoureth me with their lips; but their heart is far from me.

A man of an evil heart does not hear God, neither does he know him. He is not acquainted with God and he cannot understand God's warnings. He does not feel the move of God, neither does he respond to God's instructions because he is too far away from God. How close are you to God? When God speaks, do you hear him? When God speaks, His children hear Him.

6. NOT PREPARED TO SEEK GOD

> **2 Chronicles 12:14**
> And he did evil, because he prepared not his heart to seek the LORD.

A man of evil heart is not interested in God neither is he ready to seek God. He has his own way of dealing with issues of his life. Many people find it hard to humble themselves and seek God. They are not ready to confess their sins and seek God. Do you seek God over issues of your life or do you prefer to follow the way of the world? If 'yes,' you need another heart.

7. DARKENED

> **Romans 1:21**
> Because that, when they knew God, they glorified him not as God, neither were thankful; but became vain in their imaginations, and their foolish heart was darkened.

It is engulfed in ignorance. It can't see the light of God. It operates under deception. A man of evil heart follows a path of destruction but he does not know. He can't see that he has made a choice of death. He lives under self-deception. He will soon regret his action.

8. UNBELIEVING

> **Hebrews 3:12**
> Take heed, brethren, lest there be in any of you an evil heart of unbelief, in departing from the living God.

A man of evil heart does not follow God because he does not believe Him. He cannot trust God for his deliverance, neither can he trust Him for his provision. Every little challenge demoralises him. Do you believe what God says concerning you? If you believe, then you will act it out.

9. DOUBLE-HEARTED

> **Psalm 12:2**
> They speak vanity every one with his neighbour: with flattering lips and with a double heart do they speak.

The man with an evil heart says one thing while meaning another. A man of an evil heart is never real. He cannot be genuine. He is not dependable and his word is untrustworthy. Do you have integrity? If not, it could be that you are double-hearted and must have failed many people.

10. PROUD

> **Jeremiah 48:29**
> We have heard the pride of Moab, (he is exceeding proud) his loftiness, and his arrogancy, and his pride, and the haughtiness of his heart.

A man of evil heart is proud and exalts himself above measure. He idolises himself. His destruction is in his heart. He will soon find himself in a river he cannot swim because he will ignore warnings. How humble are you? God gives grace only to the humble but He will personally resist the proud.

11. REBELLIOUS

> **Jeremiah 5:23**
> But this people hath a revolting and a rebellious heart; they are revolted and gone.

A man of an evil heart is rebellious. He always finds faults in the deeds of other people. He accuses people of sin he himself is committing. He will soon organise how to overthrow the establishment of another man. Do you always find faults in your leaders or do you pray for them? If you always find faults in those whom God has placed above you, then, you are a rebellious person and you need to change before the devil uses you to plot evil.

12. MAD

> **Ecclesiastes 9:3**
> This is an evil among all things that are done under the sun, that there is one event unto all: yea, also the heart of the sons of men is full of evil, and madness is in their heart while they live, and after that they go to the dead.

A man of an evil heart practices madness unknowingly. Due to lack of connection to the spirit of God, he has no sound mind which the Holy Spirit gives to believers. He does shameful things and glory in them. He lacks capacity to make Godly decision and to differentiate between good and evil. He displays foolishness and calls it wisdom. He will sow evil seed and expect good harvest. He is mad in all his ways. He cannot make Godly judgement in any situation. These days, people walk around half-naked and call it fashion. They are displaying madness of the heart. Are you biblically mad or are you normal? If you are naked and not feel ashamed, then, you are not normal. It is the way of old creature, not the new. Only a mad man can boast against the Almighty God. Only the mad can boast in committing error. It is only a mad man who can worship himself instead of the everlasting God and boast of tomorrow that he does not know. It takes a mad man to live in this temporary world without critically considering his end despite seeing how the world is swallowing its own people.

The Mind of an Evil Heart

The heart determines the desires a man will develop. The type of heart you have will determine the types of your desires.

> **Psalms 37:4**
> Delight thyself also in the LORD; and he shall give thee the desires of thine heart.

The mind is the part of a man that thinks reasons and judges situations. It is the faculty of thinking, reasoning and applying knowledge. The mind determines the action after all the reasoning, thinking and judgement have been made. The desire in the heart will be communicated to the mind to determine how it functions. A man of an evil heart will definitely have an evil (carnal) mind. You cannot have an evil heart and have Godly mind.

How Does a Carnal Mind Function?

1. **WORLDLY IN OPERATION:**

> **1 Corinthians 3:3**
> For ye are yet carnal: for whereas there is among you envying, and strife, and divisions, are ye not carnal, and walk as men?

The carnally minded man is selfish and worldly in both feeling and conduct. His thoughts and reasoning are about glorifying the satisfaction of the flesh. Such kind of mind does not think about heaven or God but only about how to possess this world. The carnal man chases things that will not last, like a chase after the wind. If you only think about this world and its brief enjoyment, you are not yet a new creature.

2. INSENSITIVE TO SHAME

> **Romans 1:28**
> And even as they did not like to retain God in their knowledge, God gave them over to a reprobate mind, to do those things which are not convenient...

A reprobate mind does shameful things without feeling ashamed. Since he glories in shameful things, such a man can be proud of sleeping with someone of the same sex. He does not see anything wrong in certain habits that are dishonourable. He has no sensitivity to what is permissible and not permissible. Without the Holy Spirit, no man can be genuinely convinced of his wrong.

3. ENEMY OF GOD

> **Romans 8:7**
> Because the carnal mind is enmity against God: for it is not subject to the law of God, neither indeed can be.

Due to lack of the Holy-Spirit, a carnal man does not submit to the authority of God. He does not obey or honour God.

He forms an independent government for himself and lives under his own authority. If you operate your life with your own principles and ideas, you are not yet a new creature.

4. PRODUCES A WASTEFUL LIFE

Ephesians 4: 17
This I say therefore, and testify in the Lord, that ye henceforth walk not as other Gentiles walk, in the vanity of their mind.

Vanity of mind means empty thoughts that will produce a wasteful life. A man of carnal mind does not recognise God or seek for the purpose of his existence. He lives a life of waste; a life that does not benefit his creator. He lives only for himself and his place shall be remembered no more. Are you living for yourself or for your creator? If you are still living for yourself, then, you are not yet a new creature.

5. PRODUCES WICKED WORKS

Colossians 1:21
And you, that were sometime alienated and enemies in your mind by wicked works, yet now hath he reconciled.

A carnal mind thinks and generates decisions that will lead to a wicked work. Thoughts of his mind are very hostile to God because of its wicked nature. When a carnal man is offended, the thoughts over the offence will generate a decision that will lead to wicked action such as revenge, malice, wishing other people evil etc. When a carnal man thinks about a business, the decision to handle it will involve wickedness such as manipulating the system and deception. Do you get involved in deception or do things that will make other people cry? Does the dream you are chasing affect other people negatively? If yes, you are not yet the new creature that God is seeking.

6. IMPURITY

> **Titus 1:15**
> Unto the pure all things are pure: but unto them that are defiled and unbelieving is nothing pure; but even their mind and conscience is defiled.

The mind and conscience of a carnal man are being defiled and every outward work that proceeds from them is unclean also. He loves and practises evil and he is constantly growing worse. A carnal mind produces dirty thoughts and work as stated in Galatians 5:19-21. He is always unclean according to the way of the old creature.

The Character of an Evil Heart

Character describes your behaviour which could be directly linked to the nature of your heart and mind. It could also be linked to the type of spirit that is sponsoring the behaviour of a carnal man. A spirit is identified by the kind of work it is producing. An evil heart is under the guidance of an evil spirit which will produce bad character in its victim.

> **John 10:10**
> The thief cometh not, but for to steal, and to kill, and to destroy: I am come that they might have life, and that they might have it more abundantly.

The three-fold mission of the devil is to steal, or kill or destroy. He carries out his mission by influencing the behaviour of man. After carefully studying the nature of the heart of a man, he decides which kind of spirit will be suitable to send into his life to make him to exhibit a behaviour that will enable him (the devil) to carry out his mission in the individual's life. One of the major spirits the devil uses in the life of an un-regenerated man is the spirit of strife that will generate enmity. The devil is on the mission of creating enmity that will create an opportunity for him to achieve his mission. There are three kinds of enmity the devil uses to carry out his mission.

A. ENMITY BETWEEN MAN AND GOD

The devil always wants to make man an enemy of God by manipulating him to go against God. He achieves this through:

1. The spirit of disobedience

He manipulates man to disobey God's instruction so as to turn man against God.

> **Ephesians 2:2**
> Wherein in time past ye walked according to the course of this world, according to the prince of the power of the air, the spirit that now worketh in the children of disobedience.

Whenever you choose to disobey God, you must know that you are directly cooperating with the devil. When a man disobeys God, he is separated from Him and he becomes vulnerable. This makes it easier for the devil to carry out his mission in the life of the man. The devil will then be able to steal or destroy or kill as the situation favours him. It is the same spirit he used to turn God against Adam and Eve in the Garden of Eden. He succeeded in robbing them of divine association which they had enjoyed for a long time. If you are a new creature, still disobeying God, you must know that you are directly positioning yourself as an enemy of God. This may enable the devil to carry out his mission in any area of your life. I pray that every hole you have created in your armour shall be sealed up today by the blood of Jesus.

2. Spirit of the anti-Christ

The devil sends this spirit into the life of a man who has an evil heart to make the person oppose anything that is of the Lord Jesus Christ. Such a man never confesses Christ as his personal Lord.

> **1 John 4:3**
> And every spirit that confesseth not that Jesus Christ is come in the flesh is not of God: and this is that spirit of antichrist, whereof ye have heard that it should come; and even now already is it in the world.

This is also the spirit that sponsors religious activities without involving Jesus Christ. The devil deceives people that they can get to God through their own chosen ways. Such men claim to obey God because of their good works but ignore Jesus. Unknowingly they have made themselves enemies of God. Good works without Jesus end in hell. Every good work of man is like dirty rags. The good work will be acceptable unto God and yield dividends only if it is done in the name of Jesus Christ. You can never be heavenly good without Jesus. No other foundation can any man lay apart from the one lay by God Almighty. Accepting the entrance of the spirit of the anti-Christ into your life will allow the devil to carry out his mission in your life.

B. ENMITY BETWEEN MAN AND MAN

The devil wants to make man an enemy of another man. He influences men to behave wrongly towards each other once he notices that they have evil hearts. He does this through:

The spirit of jealousy and envy.

This is the root of murderous and every devilish behaviour.

> **Proverbs 27:4**
> Wrath is cruel, and anger is outrageous; but who is able to stand before envy?

Envy is longing to possess something awarded to or achieved by another person. An envious person feels unhappy about the achievement of another person. Also, jealousy makes you feel angry towards the success of another man. It is the work of the flesh. It belongs to the old creature. When the spirit of jealousy and envy take root in the heart of a man, he starts behaving in an evil manner towards the person he is envious of. This will invite series of evil suggestions and motivations that may result in intense hatred that invites murder.

If you suffer from envy and jealousy, you will always be an enemy of fellow human beings. People will soon discover that whenever they achieve success, you always feel angry so, they will move away from you. When this seed of hatred towards other people's achievement takes root in your heart, you have created an opportunity for the devil to carry out his mission. He may steal your joy or your health or kill whatever he is able to kill in any area of your life. Through jealousy, King Saul became an enemy of David (**1 Samuel 18:9**). After sometime, he lost his life. Through jealousy, Cain killed Abel (***Genesis 4***) and he received a divine curse upon his life. Where there is envy and jealousy, there will be rivalry between people and they get divided. People commit series of sins because they want to be like someone else. People show anger without cause due to envy. People are divided because they are in competition with each other.

There are people whose interests are the possessions of other people. It is the spouse of another person that appears suitable to them. It is the job of another person that they want. They prefer the clothes another man puts on. This is the root cause of every manner of evil among humanity. Today, people are divided and hate each other due to envy and jealousy. At least 10 out of the 17 works of the flesh are connected to envy (***Galatians 5:17-19***). May God protect your heart and mind against the invasion of the spirit of envy and jealousy in Jesus' name.

C. ENMITY WITHIN A MAN

This is man as an enemy of himself. The devil makes man to hate himself by influencing him to behave wrongly towards himself. He achieves this through:

1. The Spirit of self-destructive habit

This is the spirit that makes man to engage in a habit that will destroy him or her. This spirit manifest, through seduction. This spirit makes man to do things that he or she will not naturally do. The spirit creates a convincing reason in a man so that he or she can engage in a destructive habit.

> **1 Timothy 4:1**
> Now the Spirit speaketh expressly, that in the latter times some shall depart from the faith, giving heed to seducing spirits, and doctrines of devils.

Through the seducing spirit, men have practiced idolatry (***2 Kings 21:9***), committed adultery (***Numbers 25:1***), and listened to false doctrine (***Mark 13:22***) among others sins which they would not have committed naturally. All these habits will open the door for the devil to carry out his mission in people's lives. For example, those that committed adultery in Numbers 25 lost their lives in the desert. Many marriages have broken down because of false doctrine. Many live under curses because they have gotten involved in the worshiping of idols. Only those who hate themselves can do such things. If you allow the devil to seduce you to do things you will not do ordinarily, then you need to check your salvation, if truly you have been regenerated.

2. Fear

When the enemy attacks your mind with the spirit of fear and you accommodate it, soon fear will invite worry which leads to anxiety. Anxiety will lead to depression and results in high blood pressure. The consequences could become unimaginable. This allows the devil to carry out his mission. He can steal or destroy the health of his victim. He can take away sound mind from the person.

> **1 John 4:18**
> There is no fear in love; but perfect love casteth out fear: because fear hath torment. He that feareth is not made perfect in love.

Fear is a self-destructive habit which opens the door for the devil. It torments. This should be found among the old creatures, not the new. Only those who hate themselves give room to fear.

The Good Heart - Our New Heart

As a new creature, you have a new heart described as a good heart. The understanding of the new heart will help you to examine your heart and deal with anything that is ungodly inside of it.

Characteristics of a Good Heart

1. IT IS PURE

> **Matthew 5:8**
> Blessed are the pure in heart: for they shall see God.

A new creature has a pure heart. It is free from the dominion and pollution of sin. It does not hide offence or any ungodly thing. Even when a man of a pure heart does wrong, he does not do it intentionally. His heart is pure. Is your heart pure? Do you hide evil desire inside of it? If it is not pure, you need to wash it with the blood of Jesus. Only the pure heart will receive anointed ideas and desires that are of God.

2. IT IS LARGE

The new heart you received at the point of regeneration is a large one.

> **2 Corinthians 6:11**
> O ye Corinthians, our mouth is open unto you, our heart is enlarged.

The large heart is given so that you will be able to accommodate so many things that will come your way as a Christian. It has a large space to accommodate different kinds of things the world will throw on your way. You will be able to tolerate people and situations without complaint or criticism. If you can accommodate people irrespective of their diverse characters and reasoning, you truly have an enlarged heart. It takes an enlarged heart to be patient with people and situations irrespective of the level of irritation.

3. FILLED WITH WISDOM

A good heart has wisdom as its treasure. You are given a wise heart to enable your heart generate wise desires and your mind to be able to process good information received from the heart. It will aid you in making good judgements about issues of life. You will also be able to distinguish good from evil and make wise decisions in life.

> **Proverbs 10:8**
> The wise in heart will receive commandments: but a prating fool shall fall.

I pray that the wisdom of God will rest with you in Jesus name.

4. TREASURY OF GOOD

The heart of a new creature is filled with abundance of good things such as peace, love, kindness, etc. It has anointed ideas that can transform life. It is a heart that knows how to build. *Matthew 12:35* confirms that *'A good man out of the good treasure of the heart bringeth forth good things: and an evil man out of the evil treasure bringeth forth evil things.'* There is no situation your heart cannot handle. It has solution to every problem. When it receives illumination of the Holy Spirit, the heart of a new creature can do many wonders. May God water your heart to produce good treasures inside of it in Jesus' name.

5. DESIROUS OF GOD

The heart of a new creature always wants more of God. It is always hungry to know more of God. That is why it is easier for it to obey God's instruction always.

> **Psalms 84:2**
> My soul longeth, yea, even fainteth for the courts of the LORD: my heart and my flesh crieth out for the living God.

Do you want more of God or are you satisfied with your present spiritual situation? You need more of God because there are heights you have not yet reached in life. There are deep revelations that can only be grasped by those who are ready to go deeper with God in relationship. May God take you to a deeper level in His relationship with you in Jesus 'name.

6. PERFECT WITH GOD

A good heart is blameless before God. It operates with the spirit of excellence. It is error-free. It is a heart that will follow instruction to detail.

> **Psalms 101:2**
> I will behave myself wisely in a perfect way. O when wilt thou come unto me? I will walk within my house with a perfect heart.

This implies whole-heartedness for God, single-mindedness and sincerity. It does all things to please God always. The heart of a new creature is always above accusation. May God give you a perfect heart to do everything perfectly in Jesus' name.

7. TENDER

A good heart is soft. It is flexible. Due to its softness, it can easily change to suit the situation. It finds it easy to let go any offence against it. It easily forgives. Also, it can easily humble itself especially when it is rebuked.

> **2 Kings 22:19**
> Because thine heart was tender, and thou hast humbled thyself before the LORD, when thou heardest what I spake against this place, and against the inhabitants thereof, that

they should become a desolation and a curse, and hast rent thy clothes, and wept before me; I also have heard thee, saith the LORD.

It is a heart that can be touched by situation. It is malleable. How do you react when you are rebuked? If you find it easy to apologise and humble yourself without raising any defence, then you are really a new creature.

8. FIXED ON GOD

A new creature has a heart that is fixed only on God. Only in God does he trust without looking back. Irrespective of the changes around, a good heart remains fixed on God. It is impossible for it to doubt God.

> **Psalms 112:7**
> He shall not be afraid of evil tidings: his heart is fixed, trusting in the LORD.

As a new creature, your stand in God should not be open to negotiation. It should remain fixed on God irrespective of what is going on around you. May God give you enough grace to keep your faith intact in Jesus' name.

9. AWED BY THE WORD OF GOD

A new creature trembles when he/she hears the Word of God. A good heart does not disregard revelation neither does it ignore the word of God. The heart of a new creature shakes when he or she hear the word of God. **Psalm 119:161** says *'Princes have persecuted me without a cause: but my heart standeth in awe of thy word.'* If you are a new creature, the word of God should arrest your attention. You cannot be a new creature and ignore the word of God. May God give you ears that hear in Jesus' name.

10. CIRCUMCISED

This is the cutting off of sin and the practising of holiness. A good heart comes with inner, not outward change in a man. These are people who are Christians, not outwardly, but inwardly; in the heart and spirit, not in the letter; baptized, not with water only, but with the Holy Ghost.

> **Deuteronomy 30:6**
> And the LORD thy God will circumcise thine heart, and the heart of thy seed, to love the LORD thy God with all thine heart, and with all thy soul, that thou mayest live.

A circumcised heart loves God in totality. May God take total control of your heart in Jesus' name.

11. REJOICES IN THE LORD

A good heart rejoices in the Lord, not in man or the circumstances of his or her life. He is always rejoicing because he is a saved person. *Psalms 13:5* affirms *'But I have trusted in thy mercy; my heart shall rejoice in thy salvation.'* Only a good heart can rejoice always because its source of joy is not of this world but in the Lord of salvation. The grace to always rejoice shall locate you today in Jesus' name.

12. DEVOID OF FEAR

God is love and there is no fear in love. A good heart is bold in all situations because it has not done any evil. Fear is for law breakers, not law abiding people. As a new creature, you have nothing to be afraid of because the Lord of hosts is with you.

> **Psalms 27:3**
> Though an host should encamp against me, my heart shall not fear: though war should rise against me, in this will I be confident.

May God make you as bold as a lion in Jesus' name.

The Mind of a Good Heart

The heart develops desire and this is communicated to the mind. The mind thinks and reasons it out for a decision to be made. The nature of a heart will influence the nature of a mind and its operations. How can we describe the mind of a good heart?

1. **IT IS CHRIST-LIKE**

> **1 Corinthians 2:16**
> For who hath known the mind of the Lord, that he may instruct him? But we have the mind of Christ.

A new creature has the mind of Jesus Christ. According to **Philippians 2:5**, the mind of Christ is a mind of humility. Due to His humble nature, Jesus took the form of a servant. He preferred to serve others instead of being served. If you enjoy serving instead of being served, you have the mind of Christ. If you prefer people serving you, then, you need to pray for the mind of Christ. Jesus made himself equal to man so that people could develop a sense of equality

The NEW *Creature*

and be able to relate with him freely. Humility makes people feel equal, though, they may not be equal in terms of position. If people around you cannot freely relate with you, you are not yet a new creature. A new creature creates no barrier between himself and people around him. Jesus did not cling to His glorious position as the son of God but He released His heavenly glory and made Himself of no reputation. He lived as a mere man such that those who were far below Him had no sense of intimidation. If your relationship with people makes them feel intimidated, then, you are not yet a new creature.

The mind of Jesus was filled with the will of God. Jesus had the knowledge of God's will and He pursued it. His mind was preoccupied with doing God's will, not His own will. In **Matthew 26:39-40**, Jesus clung to God's will when it seemed inconvenient. He chose to pay the price of doing God's will. He put aside personal comfort and convenience. He never pursued His own agenda when He was in this world. He lived for God.

Are you living for God? If yes, you are a new creature. The mind of Jesus Christ was filled with the wisdom of God as stated in **James 3:17-18**. Jesus never used human wisdom. His action always produced the fruit of righteousness. A new creature with the mind of Christ operates with Godly wisdom. His action and decision produce righteousness, peace and joy.

The mind of Christ is filled with the knowledge of real holiness and its beauties. Holiness is always attractive to Him. If you have the mind of Christ, you will always love holiness because it will always be attractive to you. If you find holiness burdensome, you are not yet a new creature. The mind of Christ is filled with the principles of God. A new creature does not develop his own principles for life but operates in that of God. As a new creature, you are not allowed to have your own principles but live in that of God. You can no longer do as you consider appropriate but as God's principles dictate.

2 Timothy 1:7 states that we have been given a sound mind. It is a mind with self-control. It is a disciplined mind. It functions properly. It is void of madness. As a new creature, your mind should maintain its shape irrespective of challenges. You should not be out of your mind because of difficulty. You should be able to maintain the sanity of your mind despite any confrontation. Even on the cross, Jesus still won a soul. Nothing was able to make Him lose His mind. Nothing could change His focus.

A sound mind does not do what it would not do naturally, irrespective of the situation; it is constant. Poverty and lack cannot make it to steal because it has never stolen before. It cannot be enticed or seduced into immorality because it does not harbour such seed. If you conform just to suit the situation of life, you are not yet a new creature. If you have to lie and manipulate because of fear, you are not yet a new creature. May God's grace be multiplied upon you in Jesus' name.

2. FILLED WITH WISE THOUGHTS

The mind of a good heart thinks wisely. The kind of things it thinks about increase its wisdom. As a new creature, there are certain things you should think about that will make you wiser. If your heart produces wise desires, your mind should think wisely. Examples of wise thoughts are:

1. **Thoughts about God's love**

> **Psalms 48:9**
> We have thought of thy lovingkindness, O God, in the midst of thy temple.

When you think about God's love to you, you will never do anything that will break God's heart. You will always be willing to do God's will as a way of pay-back. Also, if you think about God's love, you will be free from guilt and deception of the accuser (the devil).The knowledge of His love will make you to confess that truly nothing can separate you from God because His love never fails. When the enemy says that God has forsaken you, you will not be moved.

2. **Thoughts about the purpose of chastisement**

> **Deuteronomy 8:5**
> Thou shalt also consider in thine heart, that, as a man chasteneth his son, so the LORD thy God chasteneth thee.

God is a father to you, so He sometime chastises His children to correct them and put them on the right path in life. His chastisement comes in different ways and forms. It could come as a certain challenge that refuses to depart until God's appointed time. In *Numbers 12:12-15*, God chastised Miriam and for seven days she was leprous. Nothing could help her until the time God had specified passed.

If you face challenges that defy all solutions, it may be that God is chastising you. There will always be a reason why certain difficulty persists in your life. Check it out. It is one thing to be chastised, it is another thing to get the message God is passing across to you. You must think about all your difficulties and understand why God allowed them and the lessons to learn from the experience. It will make you wiser and help you not to keep on making the same mistake over and over.

3. Thoughts of the past

> **Deuteronomy 32:7**
> Remember the days of old, consider the years of many generations: ask thy father, and he will shew thee; thy elders, and they will tell thee.

There are lessons to learn from the past. A new creature thinks about the past. Your little beginning is part of your past. You must not forget your little beginning, where God picked you from. The more you think about your little beginning, the more humble you become. When you remember how little you were when God picked you up, compared with your present height, it will humble you. Your little beginning is a testimony that it was not your ability that brought you to your present level. Those who boast of their present achievement have forgotten the past. They forgot that they were not great in the past but were very little.

A new creature thinks of the past. Moreover, part of history could be what you witnessed God doing in somebody else's life. If you remember how God paid somebody back in the past, it will give you wisdom on how to handle your situation today. A wise man learns from somebody else's calamity to avoid it in his own life.

4. **Thoughts about the latter end**

> **Deuteronomy 32:29**
> O that they were wise, that they understood this, that they would consider their latter end!

The mind of a new creature thinks about the end. Whatever he is doing, he considers the end. As a new creature, you must always think about the end of whatever you are doing. Consider what will happen to you after you finish your education, how you will end your career or how you will end your ministry. The end is a reality and as you consider it, the light of God illuminates your mind to know God's plan for the end of what you are doing or where you are going.

The exit point is very important in all human endeavours. You must be careful how you end a relationship because tomorrow is unclear. You must be careful how you end an employment because you never know what the future holds. Always ask yourself how you will end it. Also ask yourself what your end would be. What legacy will you leave behind? What memory will you create in people's mind? May your end be glorious in Jesus' name. May your memory in people's mind be sweet in Jesus' name.

5. **Thoughts about Divine provisions**

> **1 Samuel 12:24**
> Only fear the LORD, and serve him in truth with all your heart: for consider how great things he hath done for you.

The mind of a new creature thinks about the blessings and provisions of God. When a man thinks about blessings and provisions of God, his faith will be strengthened to face tomorrow's challenges. He will have confidence that if God can provide for him today, He will also provide for him tomorrow. With this confidence, you will be able to start a new project or pursue a new dream no matter how big it seems. God never changes (***Hebrews 13:8***), as He is doing today, so He will do, even more, tomorrow. The more you think in this way, the wiser you become and your decisions will be of God's wisdom. May your mind be strengthened by the wisdom of God in Jesus' name.

6. Thoughts about God's wonderful deeds:

Job 37:14
Hearken unto this, O Job: stand still, and consider the wondrous works of God.

The mind of a new creature thinks about God's wonderful works to tap wisdom from them. The deeds of God reveal His power and wisdom. His works will communicate the power of your creator into your mind. Think about the stars and the firmament. Since the days they were all created, none has been lost. The power of God keeps them in their position. The weather knows when and how to change. The sun and the stars reveal the glory of God.

With these thoughts in your mind, you will tell yourself that God who created all these wonderful things has more than enough power to handle every situation in your life. His works reveal His unlimited ability. Your mind gets strengthened and you will be able to say that indeed power belongs to God. There is a lot to learn from the deeds of God.

7. Thoughts of God's interest in man

> **Psalms 8:3-5**
> When I consider thy heavens, the work of thy fingers, the moon and the stars, which thou hast ordained; What is man, that thou art mindful of him? and the son of man, that thou visitest him? For thou hast made him a little lower than the angels, and hast crowned him with glory and honour.

As a new creature, you must think in your mind the divine interest of God in man. Despite the fact that man was created from dust, God has a lot of interest in man. With all the inherent weaknesses in man, God still has pleasure in him. God relates with man and exalts him into a position of honour in His kingdom. His relationship with man reveals the level of His humility. God must be very humble to bring Himself down to such a level where He will make man His friend and share secret with him; the work of His hand. As a new creature, you must learn humility from God. You must be able to relate with people around you even if they are your servants. If God can relate well with man whom He created from dust, you must be able to relate with any man irrespective of their low position. People must not feel intimidated in dealing with you. People must feel secure in your presence. May God input His nature in you in Jesus' name.

8. Thoughts of his ways

> **Haggai 1:5**
> Now therefore thus saith the LORD of hosts; Consider your ways.

The mind of a good heart thinks about his ways regularly. This will enable you to discover the root cause of your challenges. It will also enable you to predict the outcome of your action. You need to think about the situations in your life regularly so as to prepare for the future. Sometimes, you are the cause of your problem but you may be busy blaming someone else. However, if you think about your ways, God will illuminate your mind to detect the truth. Also, thinking about your ways can help you detect hidden problems. When last did you think about your life situation and ask the Holy Spirit to reveal hidden things inside of it to you?

Before you make wrong conclusions you need to think well about your ways. Think about your challenges that defy all solutions. Think carefully about why you should be facing what you are facing. It may be that you got certain things wrong in your life. You may need to adopt a new strategy in the way you handle certain matters.

9. Thoughts about nature

Matthew 6:28-31
And why take ye thought for raiment? Consider the lilies of the field, how they grow; they toil not, neither do they spin: And yet I say unto you, That even Solomon in all his glory was not arrayed like one of these. Wherefore, if God so clothe the grass of the field, which today is, and tomorrow is cast into the oven, shall he not much more clothe you, O ye of little faith? Therefore take no thought, saying, What shall we eat? or, What shall we drink? or, Wherewithal shall we be clothed?

A new creature thinks about nature. When you think about nature, you will be amazed about the level of care and provision the Almighty God made available to what He created. God in His wisdom has made provision for the survival of all created things. He has put in position how birds, grass, animals and all living things will get abundant supply of their needs. Among all that God has created, none was put in a glorious position like man. God has made provision for all your needs. The needs He has provided will outlive you. You cannot consume all the provisions of God during your lifetime.

God has made provision that will make your dream and vision come into fulfilment. He has made provision for what you will eat, wear and use during your lifetime. This will give you wisdom not to worry about tomorrow. You will not need to worry about your vision because God will never give you vision without provision first. The wise do not worry; they only pray and look unto heaven. If what you need are not with you at your present location they are definitely somewhere. You only need God to order your steps to wherever your provisions are. May God order your steps into all the provisions He has made for your life in Jesus name.

10. Thoughts about the attitude of Christ

Hebrews 12:2-3
Looking unto Jesus the author and finisher of our faith; who for the joy that was set before him endured the cross, despising the shame, and is set down at the right hand of the throne of God. For consider him that endured such contradiction of sinners against himself, lest ye be wearied and faint in your minds.

The new creatures think about their Saviour and learn from His life. When you think about the attitude and patience of Jesus under different challenges, you will be encouraged. You can draw a lot of strength from what Jesus experienced while He was on earth. He was always calm under tribulation and rejection. Nothing moved Him. If you think about Jesus and how He resisted all temptations and withstood persecution, nothing would move you. This will come out of the fact that God is always in control of your life situation, not the enemy. May God give you revelation into the person of Jesus and may the eyes of your mind be opened in Jesus name.

Testing Your Thoughts

The thoughts that will make you wiser and godly must pass some tests. If those thoughts fail the test, then, they cannot make you wiser or godly. Immediately you discover that the thoughts of your mind fail the test, you must refocus your mind on something worthy. The eight major tests your thought must pass through are in the words of God:

> **Philippians 4:8**
> Finally, brethren, whatsoever things are true, whatsoever things are honest, whatsoever things are just, whatsoever things are pure, whatsoever things are lovely, whatsoever things are of good report; if there be any virtue, and if there be any praise, think on these things.

1. TEST OF THE TRUTH

This includes truth in word, in action, and in thought. You must cherish this. Christ, our Master, is the truth and so His followers must be embodiment of truth. Don't engage your mind in thinking about what you have not established to be the truth. Certain things can never be true. For example, it can never be true that God has abandoned you or that He will accept evil because that will contradict His word. Whatever contradicts the word of God can never be true and you must not even think about it. Similarly, thinking that God will approve any action that contradicts His word can never be true. Therefore don't even think about it.

2. TEST OF HONESTY

This requires integrity. No double standard. Do not engage your mind in thinking about deceptive things. Let your yes be yes; do not think about lying. Ensure that the thought of your mind is always about honesty, not deception. Dishonest thoughts will soon produce deceptive character. You only need to lie once for you to continue to lie. Dishonesty will contaminate your mind and reduce its sensitivity to the warning of the Holy-Spirit.

3. TEST OF JUSTICE

This means thinking about strict justice in all dealings which will produce an upright life. Refrain from engaging your mind to think about how to use different scales in your dealings. Any thought of your mind that involves unrighteousness should be avoided. Do not think about how to deny people justice. It will produce in you, an action of double standard. It is a wicked thing to do.

4. TEST OF PURITY

This requires a clean heart to produce pure thought. The thought of your mind must be clean. Pure thought will make you undefiled and unspotted from the world. Thinking about offence will make your mind impure. Likewise thoughts of revenge will contaminate your mind. Avoid all thoughts that involve committing sin. You are a peculiar person and so must your thought be. An impure thought will produce an impure person full of series of malpractices.

5. TEST OF LOVE

This involves thoughts that will produce deeds that spring from love and also inspire love in others. There is thought that will make you to be a blessing to somebody. There is a thought that will make you to appreciate and value a fellow human being. Learn how to thank God for people around you irrespective of their behaviour towards you. After all, if God did not sanction it that you will know them, they would not have come into your life. There must be some good reasons why God allowed you to know them. Just thank God for their lives and do well to them and leave the rest for God. Think of blessing somebody and teach the person how to love through your action.

6. TEST OF GOOD REPORT

This is a life of which no evil thing can be truthfully said. Think about an action of good reputation. Avoid engaging your mind in thoughts that will produce an action which attracts negative reaction from good people. If your thoughts will not lead to good testimony, avoid it. It is a good report to hear that where you once failed, you have now succeeded. It is a good report to hear that through the help you rendered to somebody, the person has experienced promotion.

7. TEST OF VIRTUE

Give your mind to things that show good attributes. Faithfulness is a virtue; give your mind to it. Hard work is a virtue; give your mind to it. Diligence is a virtue; give your mind to it. Think about such things that will show that you possess good attributes and qualities. Such thoughts advertise you positively to the world.

8. TEST OF PRAISEWORTHINESS

This implies thoughts that will produce a commendable action. It is commendable to make the weak stronger, fixing broken relationships and helping others to achieve greater success. Think about things that when you do them, good people will thank God for your life. Finally, as a new creature, any thought of your mind that cannot satisfy the above should be expunged.

6

OUR **HERITAGE** HAS CHANGED

A HERITAGE IS PASSED down from preceding generations. It could include personal characteristics or attributes, status, title, name, traditions, and possessions. Heritage could be received from birth. Also, poverty, riches, failure, success and favour could be inherited. For example, it is a heritage to die young in some families while early achievement and longevity could be inherited in another.

One major fact about heritage is that the person who receives it has done nothing to have it. Heritage is a gift, not a wage. For example, in a family where failure is a pattern, members of such family do not need to be lazy to fail in life; it will automatically happen at the appointed time, programmed by the evil forces that have been chosen from hell. Heritage is from birth. There are two sets of births. These are Adamic Birth which comes with the Adamic nature, and the Second Birth which is through Jesus Christ. This birth comes with the divine nature.

The Old Heritage—Adamic Birth

Everyone born into this world came through the Adamic route and has inherited certain things which had been

The NEW *Creature*

passed down through that family lineage. Examples of inheritance through this linage are:

1. THE ADAMIC NATURE

1 Corinthians 15:45-48 says *'And so it is written, The first man Adam was made a living soul; the last Adam was made a quickening spirit. Howbeit that was not first which is spiritual, but that which is natural; and afterward that which is spiritual. The first man is of the earth, earthy: the second man is the Lord from heaven. As is the earthy, such are they also that are earthy: and as is the heavenly, such are they also that are heavenly.'*

The Adamic nature is worldly, always chasing worldly things. Its aim is to glorify the flesh. Since man does not need to do anything to receive an inheritance, man, born with the Adamic nature, does not need training to lust over things of the flesh. He will naturally be flesh-prone. This is characteristic of the Adamic nature. **Galatians 5:19-21** says *'Now the works of the flesh are manifest, which are these; Adultery, fornication, uncleanness, lasciviousness, Idolatry, witchcraft, hatred, variance, emulations, wrath, strife, seditions, heresies, envyings, murders, drunkenness, revellings, and such like: of the which I tell you before, as I have also told you in time past, that they which do such things shall not inherit the kingdom of God.'* If you still enjoy any of the above you are not yet a new creature.

2. SIN

Everyman born into this world has inherited sin. **Isaiah 48:8** states this unequivocally – *'Yea, thou heardest* *not; yea, thou knewest not; yea, from that time that thine ear was not opened: for I knew that thou wouldest deal very treacherously, and wast called a transgressor from the womb.'*

Being a transgressor from the womb implies that the person does not need to be born into this world before knowing how to sin. Committing sin is natural to a man that is not yet born-again. Heritage does not need an effort to be possessed. It comes through birth. For example, no one taught Cain how to kill (***Genesis 4***). He killed Abel without any prior training. He inherited the murderous nature before he was born. That is why the power of God is needed to deliver a man from the bondage of sin. There is nothing in this world that can make a man sinless because he did not pick sinful habits from this world; he got it before coming into the world. Whatever is born of the flesh is sinful.

3. SPIRITUAL BLINDNESS

Every man born into this world came with a veil which he has inherited. No matter how educated a man is, if he has no salvation, he is blind and short-sighted. He has a veil that needs to be removed. He is not ignorant because of what he has done but because he inherited it. That is why Jesus said no one can come unto him unless God draws the person. Only God can remove the veil. However, there is hope in **2 Corinthians 3:14-16** thus: *'But their minds were blinded: for until this day remaineth the same vail untaken away in the reading of the old testament; which vail is done away in Christ. But even unto this day, when Moses is read, the vail is upon their heart. Nevertheless when it shall turn to the Lord, the vail shall be taken away.'*

4. CURSES ARE BLOCKERS OF BLESSINGS

Every man born into this world has inherited curses. That is why an unbeliever does not need to invite or do evil before evil happens to him or her. Evil does not need any invitation before coming into his or her life. An accursed person lives with evil. **Galatians 3:10** confirms that: *'For as many as are of the works of the law are under the curse: for it is written, Cursed is every one that continueth not in all things which are written in the book of the law to do them.'* An accursed person does not need to do wrong things before situations in his life go wrong; and things will definitely go wrong, it is only a matter of time. Where a curse is in operation, poverty, sickness and all manners of evil reign.

This is the inheritance of the unsaved man.

5. GENERATIONAL SEEDS

Every man will produce his own kind as stated in **Genesis 1:11**. A sick man will give birth to a sick child. **2 Kings 5:27** gives us an example – *'The leprosy therefore of Naaman shall cleave unto thee, and unto thy seed for ever. And he went out from his presence a leper as white as snow.'* The above indicates that every child born by Gehazi would have leprosy. The genes of leprosy would automatically enter into their blood stream. The children would not need to do anything to have leprosy; it was their inheritance. It is only in Jesus that such a thing can be removed. If you still experience the sickness that used to trouble your parents, it means you are not yet a new creature. I pray that every genetic deformation in your life shall be corrected today in Jesus' name.

6. GENERATIONAL PATTERN

The spirit that operated in the lives of parents will automatically enter into the lives of their children. It is an inheritance. The spirit will exercise right over the children because they come from its captives. The spirit will travel from generation to generation. It could be the spirit of poverty or infirmity. Such children do not need to do anything to exhibit poverty or infirmity.

Genesis 11:30 says 'But Sarai was barren; she had no child'. This continued in *Genesis 25:21*: 'And Isaac intreated the LORD for his wife, because she was barren: and the LORD was intreated of him, and Rebekah his wife conceived.'

Also in *Genesis 29:31* 'And when the LORD saw that Leah was hated, he opened her womb: but Rachel was barren.' The above shows how the pattern and spirit of barrenness passed down from Sarah to Isaac and to Jacob. The three generations exhibited a pattern. There was nothing Isaac or his wife Rebekah did to be barren. Heritage requires no effort from the receiver; it will be automatically handed down. If you still exhibit an evil pattern in your family lineage, you are not yet a new creature. I pray that every remnant of evil pattern remaining in any area of your life shall be wiped off today in Jesus name.

New Heritage—New birth

John 3:3-6
Jesus answered and said unto him, Verily, verily, I say unto thee, Except a man be born again, he cannot see the kingdom of God. Nicodemus saith unto him, How can a man

> be born when he is old? can he enter the second time into his mother's womb, and be born? Jesus answered, Verily, verily, I say unto thee, Except a man be born of water and of the Spirit, he cannot enter into the kingdom of God. That which is born of the flesh is flesh; and that which is born of the Spirit is spirit.

As a new creature, you have been born-again, a birth through Jesus Christ as Saviour. The day you became born-again, you were given a heritage totally different from the former one in the Adamic birth. You need to have an understanding of your heritage so that you lay claim to them and reject any attempt of the enemy to manipulate you into living with the Adamic heritage. As stated before, you do not need to struggle for any heritage; the new heritage has been made ready for you by your saviour Jesus Christ. Your only responsibility is to take advantage of the new heritage presented to you.

Heritage of a New Creature

1. DIVINE NATURE

> **2 Peter 1:4**
> Whereby are given unto us exceeding great and precious promises: that by these ye might be partakers of the divine nature, having escaped the corruption that is in the world through lust.

The divine nature is the nature of God who saved you through His son Jesus Christ. God is holy and righteous. Those who claim to be His children should naturally live a holy life. As a new creature, you are not supposed to struggle to exhibit this nature because the son of a dog does not need to be trained to be like dog because what makes it dog is inside of it. As a child of God you are not supposed to find it hard to behave like God. It should be a natural thing that you exhibit the nature of God. It should not be a surprise that you love holiness because that is who you are by nature and you can't do otherwise. This is what has been handed over to you by Jesus when He was here on earth. What should be unnatural for you is to love sin because it is the heritage of another family- the Adamic. If you are still struggling with holiness your claim that you are a new creature is questionable.

2. POWER

Acts 1:8
But ye shall receive power, after that the Holy Ghost is come upon you: and ye shall be witnesses unto me both in Jerusalem, and in all Judaea, and in Samaria, and unto the uttermost part of the earth.

The Holy Spirit is an agent of regeneration. The day you became born-again, it was the Holy Spirit that orchestrated it. As a new creature, the Holy Spirit dwells inside of you. His presence manifests through the demonstration of divine ability and power. The power is given through the Holy-Spirit so that you will be able to influence the situations of your life as you desire. This power is a heritage; you have done nothing to receive it. The only qualification to receiving this power is yielding to the Lord. As a new creature, you do not need to struggle to demonstrate the power of the Holy Spirit. Your responsibility is to decree a thing and then wait and see how it will be established. You do not need to reason out how what you decree will be established; you just issue a decree in accordance with the living Word of God. Avoid being 'realistic' when you want to operate in the supernatural. When the supernatural comes into operation, the natural is set aside and reality is overthrown. Power is your heritage. When you operate in this power, you step up into the realm of the supernatural and your word becomes law. May the power of the Almighty God overshadow you in Jesus' name.

3. KINGDOM VIRTUES

> **Romans 14:17**
> For the kingdom of God is not meat and drink; but righteousness, and peace, and joy in the Holy Ghost.

Every child born into the kingdom of God inherits the three virtues of the kingdom which are: righteousness, peace and Joy. These are the heritage of the kingdom. Righteousness gives you justification in the sight of God. It qualifies you to have access to the blessings of God and His throne. You are no longer seen as an outcast but as a genuine son of the kingdom. This enables you to ignore any accusation the enemy might bring to rob you of God's blessings. If the enemy wants to accuse your mind with guilt whenever you come before the throne of God, you can shut him down by reminding him that you have not come in your own righteousness but in that of God. Justification gives power over guilt and condemnation. Peace handed over to you reconciles you to God and also gives you rest from all the troubles of life. It is a divine peace. You do not need to let the enemy rob you of peace using threat and fear. Whatever the situation, you must always have peace. After all, if God is with you, who can be against you? Joy handed over to you as a heritage has its origin in heaven, not on earth. The world does not have joy but only happiness, which is as a result of the arrangement of circumstances or happenstance. When circumstances change, the world will lose all its happiness and return to sadness. For you, however, whatever the situation, you must always rejoice because your treasures are stored in heaven, not on earth. These are virtues handed over to you as a new creature.

4. GRACE

2 Corinthians 9:8 gives a kingdom assurance thus: *'And God is able to make all grace abound toward you; that ye, always having all sufficiency in all things, may abound to every good work.'* It enables you to bear all the challenges of life. Grace is given to you to enable you to complete every good work you embark on. There is no project you can't handle in life because grace will always be available to enable you. There is no race you can't finish because the grace of God is upon you to enable you complete every race.

As a new creature, you should not be afraid of putting your hand into big projects and visions because you already have upon your life the grace. You do not need to do anything to have grace. It is already in you. What you should do is to press on without the option of quitting. As you do, grace will make you not to have regard to any challenge on the way. Mountains will be nothing before you. You will focus your attention on what is ahead of you, not what the enemy has brought to distract you. You will be amazed how far you will go. That is grace. It is a heritage. If you can rely on grace, you will always achieve success where others failed.

5. SECURITY

The Lord is your security. There is affirmation of this, thus – *'There shall no evil befall thee, neither shall any plague come nigh thy dwelling'* (**Psalm 91:10**).

God has made provision for every child that will be born into his kingdom. This implies that God knew ahead of time that there will be threatening and unpalatable situations that will come against His children. He knew that there are certain forces of evil that will attempt to threaten and terrorise His children; so He made provision for their security. Your security is not in your hands but in God's. He has given you a heritage of security. Those who came before you enjoyed this provision.

Daniel was secured in the den of lions. The three Hebrews (*Daniel 3*) were fully protected inside the fiery fire. The big fish that swallowed Jonah could not digest him because of the adequate security God had provided for him. With all the access King Saul had to weapons of warfare, he could not kill little David because the security of God upon David could not be faulted. As a new creature, do not let the concern for security imprison the good ideas God has given to you. Try new things. Do big things. Face big projects. Explore the unfamiliar. God has secured your life for Himself. Nothing can kill you until the time God has allotted to you expires.

6. TOTAL PROSPERITY

The mind of God concerning you was expressed again in *3 John 2* thus: *'Beloved, I wish above all things that thou mayest prosper and be in health, even as thy soul prospereth.'* To prosper means to succeed and flourish. God has made provisions for you to prosper both spiritually and materially. The ability to prosper entered into you the day you became born-again.

> **Zechariah 4:6**
> Then he answered and spake unto me, saying, This is the word of the LORD unto Zerubbabel, saying, Not by might, nor by power, but by my spirit, saith the LORD of hosts.

The spirit of God that dwells in you is an agent of prosperity. There are spiritual forces that determine success in life. Success is not only about what you are able to do well. There are unseen forces that affect success. For little David to defeat mighty Goliath, there must have been some unseen forces that were in operation in favour of David. For Gideon and few Israelites to blow the trumpet and defeat a mighty army, there must have been some unseen forces that went into operation in their favour. You were not born into the kingdom of God to wear yourself out because of prosperity. Prosperity has been made your heritage. Your responsibility is to rely on the Spirit of God that determines prosperity.

> **Proverbs 3:6**
> In all thy ways acknowledge him, and he shall direct thy paths.

7. VICTORY

> **1 Corinthians 15:57**
> But thanks be to God, which giveth us the victory through our Lord Jesus Christ.

Every battle you will face in life as a child of God has been won for you by Jesus Christ. You are no longer expected to fight any battle again if the battle has already been won.

> **2 Chronicles 20:15**
> And he said, Hearken ye, all Judah, and ye inhabitants of Jerusalem, and thou king Jehoshaphat, Thus saith the LORD unto you, Be not afraid nor dismayed by reason of this great multitude; for the battle is not yours, but God's.

Jesus gave you victory when He died and resurrected. He conquered death, poverty, sickness, sin, curses and every manner of forces of evil both spiritual and human. You don't need to fight them again.

The only battle you will lose is the one you have decided to fight by yourself.

Victory is a heritage. Battles have been won for you so, you don't need to fight any battle again. When you face any challenge, release it unto the Lord. Don't waste your resources by fighting a defeated and annihilated army or multitude. Face every battle from the side of victory, not defeat. You are facing a battle from the side of victory when you release it unto the Lord and you start praising God for imminent victory. It will be an error and act of disobedience for you to start fighting for yourself when you have been told that the battle is of the Lord. May you wax stronger than your enemy in Jesus 'name.

Facts about Heritage

While it is true that you have been given a heritage by God, it is important to know certain facts about heritage.

1. HERITAGE COULD BE LOST

Whatever is not properly kept could be lost. This is because there are thieves looking for the blessings of others to steal. For example in *Genesis 3*, Adam and Eve lost the Garden of Eden which God gave to them as a heritage due to disobedience. They took the fruit God did not give them and lost the garden God gave them. When you bring into your life what God has not given you, you give an access to the devil, the thief, to come into your life to steal what God has given you. In *1 Samuel 15*, King Saul lost the throne that was given to him as a gift by God. He lost it due to disobedience.

At the outset, the humility of his heart qualified him to have the throne but after sometime he became arrogant to everybody including God who made him king. He lost the throne he got freely. He also lost his sanity. When you stop doing what brought you to the top, you start moving downward in life. In *1 Samuel 2:30*, the house of Eli lost their heritage due to wickedness. They ignored God's warning. They provoked God to anger. You can't have the blessings of God without God. The day you start dishonouring God, you start sending God's blessings out of your life because His blessings will only stay where He is honoured.

2. HERITAGE COULD BE SOLD

Like in everything with God, you have a choice. In *Genesis 25:33*, Esau sold his inheritance for a morsel of meat. He exchanged his inheritance for food. He despised his heritage and sold it. Whenever you find yourself under pressure, don't enter into any negotiation. Do not take decisions when you are weak and tired. The devil is crafty; he knows when you are vulnerable. He knows that you can't make quality decision when you are hungry and weak, so he will attempt to lure you into situations that require urgent decision when you are weak.

Many have exchanged their heritage unknowingly due to the pressure of the moment. Also, you must know when to flee. Joseph fled from the presence of Mrs Potiphar in *Genesis 39*; otherwise he would have exchanged his greatness for few minutes of sex. Some people have exchanged their victory for adultery. They got involved in adultery which caused them to lose their victory. Some people exchanged their joy for temporary sinful enjoyment. Some people have lost power while some have lost peace due to evil transactions. Heritage could be sold. May God's grace multiply upon your life in Jesus 'name. May you never sell your heritage in Jesus 'name.

3. HERITAGE COULD BE WASTED

In *Luke 15*, the prodigal son took his heritage and went to a far place and wasted it due to reckless lifestyle. The world gathered round him and made themselves his friends. He did not know that riches have wings and they do fly away. He lost his self-control and he lost everything. The wise know that saving is needed for the unknown future. Do not waste your possession. Don't waste your open door. Don't waste what God has given you. Don't waste precious time. A careless lifestyle will waste your blessings. Heritage needs protection and management. Take care of what God has given you. Don't spoil the opportunities God creates for you. Don't corrupt yourself with destructive behaviour or possession. Don't waste your strength. May God make you wiser to know what to avoid and what to embrace in Jesus' name.

4. HERITAGE COULD INCREASE

You can advance in power. You can experience more joy. You can move from glory to glory. Your peace can multiply and flow like a river. In *Acts 3*, Peter healed the sick by word and body contact but in *Act 5:15*, he was healing through shadow contact. He advanced in power. You can possess more territory. The more you bring yourself under the dominion of the Holy Spirit, the more you rise in life. The more you increase in faith, the more you exercise dominion over life. The more you increase your closeness to God, the more you operate in the supernatural. May you move from glory to glory. May God make you greater than your expectations. You are a new creature and that is what you shall remain.

7

OUR LIVES HAVE CHANGED

AS A NEW CREATURE you have received a new life through Jesus Christ. The old lifestyle is gone. Jesus brought to us a new life. We need to be constantly reminded about the new life we have received so that we will not be tempted to drift into the old life. What kind of life did we live before we became a new creatures? What kind of life should we live now as new creatures?

1. SELF-SEEKING VERSUS GOD-SEEKING

The old life is self-seeking. It is full of sin and passion for a life of sin. It pursues selfishness.

> **2 Corinthians 5:15**
> And that he died for all, that they which live should not henceforth live unto themselves, but unto him which died for them, and rose again.

The natural man lives for himself, not God. On the other hand, the new life is God-seeking. It is full of righteousness and passion for holiness.

> **Galatians 6:8**
> For he that soweth to his flesh shall of the flesh reap corruption; but he that soweth to the Spirit shall of the Spirit reap life everlasting.

Those who are God-seeking will reap everlasting life. Are you self-seeking or God-seeking? Do you promote your own interest or that of God? The new creature is God-seeking.

2. MAN-LIKE VERSUS CHRIST-LIKE

The old life is man-like. It behaves like mere man. The natural man talks like man and reasons like man. On the other hand, the new life is Christ-like. It carries the nature of Jesus and operates like Jesus in all situations. The new creature operates with the identity God has given, not the one from the world.

> **2 Corinthians 4:10**
> Always bearing about in the body the dying of the Lord Jesus, that the life also of Jesus might be made manifest in our body.

The life of Jesus is the life of the supernatural. The new creature is Jesus-like in action not man-like. It is full of heavenly ambitions. It manifests the life of Jesus, not only in the body but also in the demonstration of power.

3. CONFORMED LIFE VERSUS TRANSFORMED LIFE

The old life has no shape of its own. It adjusts to the shape given by situations. It is a conformed life. Life dictates to it.

Always, it adjusts to suit the prevailing situation. The new life is transformed. It has a settled shape. It dictates to the situation. As a new creature you are supposed to dictate to every challenge of your life. You are supposed to tell the enemy where he belongs. You are not supposed to adjust to accommodate sickness, lack, hatred, failure and every manner of evil but you must rule over them and never allow them to control your life. You must maintain and retain the shape God has given to you as a new creature. You must refuse to comply with the dictates of life's situations.

> **Psalms 8:6**
> Thou madest him to have dominion over the works of thy hands; thou hast put all things under his feet.

The above is the power God has given you and you must not negotiate it with any force. You must not allow anything to dominate you.

> **Romans 12:2**
> And be not conformed to this world: but be ye transformed by the renewing of your mind, that ye may prove what is that good, and acceptable, and perfect, will of God.

4. LACK OF SATISFACTION VERSUS SATISFACTION IN GOD

The old life has no satisfaction. Nothing satisfies it. Like a grave, it never has enough. It is never contented. That is why it is full of evil practices. The new life came with contentment. It finds satisfaction in the Lord. That is why it is full of peace.

> **John 4:14**
> But whosoever drinketh of the water that I shall give him shall never thirst; but the water that I shall give him shall be in him a well of water springing up into everlasting life.

Only the new creature has access to this water Jesus promised. The water of God gives satisfaction and it quenches thirst forever. Christ enjoins his followers in **Luke 12:15**; *'And he said unto them, Take heed, and beware of covetousness: for a man's life consisteth not in the abundance of the things which he possesseth'*.

The above indicates that nothing satisfies the natural man; not even abundant possession. **Hebrews 13:5** says *'Let your conversation be without covetousness; and be content with such things as ye have: for he hath said, I will never leave thee, nor forsake thee.'* The new creatures' satisfactions are rooted in the assurance that their God will always be there for them both in the time of lack and in abundance

5. RESTLESSNESS VERSUS RESTFUL LIFE

The natural man is restless because he is always hungry for something. He does not have a good shepherd that cares for him. The new creature has a settled life because his hunger is assuaged by the Lord. He is like a sheep that has got a good shepherd who cares for its needs.

Psalms 23:1, sums it up that: *'The LORD is my shepherd; I shall not want.'* On the other hand, according to Isaiah 57:21: *'There is no peace, saith my God, to the wicked.'*

The natural man has no peace. He lives with a sense of insecurity.

> **John 14:27**
> Peace I leave with you, my peace I give unto you: not as the world giveth, give I unto you. Let not your heart be troubled, neither let it be afraid.

The new creature has divine peace. There is a sense of security because God that watches over him never slumbers. Peace is a legacy Jesus Christ left behind for the new creatures.

6. DEATH VERSUS LIFE

The old life is full of death and the fear of death rules. Death rules because there is no power to resist it. There is no resistance to death when it comes to kill hope, joy, business, marriage, health etc. In the new life that we were given, there is abundant life. We and whatever we touch lives. No more death but life. Our jobs live, our marriages live, our careers live and all that we touch live.

> **Hebrews 2:14**
> Forasmuch then as the children are partakers of flesh and blood, he also himself likewise took part of the same; that through death he might destroy him that had the power of death, that is, the devil.

The power of death has been destroyed in the new life that we received. Therefore, you can no longer fear death. It is foolishness to fear what is dead. Jesus has killed death in your life, so you don't need to be afraid of it again.

> **Hebrews 11:35**
> Women received their dead raised to life again: and others

were tortured, not accepting deliverance; that they might obtain a better resurrection.'

Women of faith with knowledge resisted death when he came to take away their love ones. They knew that they have been delivered from the power of death, so he could no longer rule their lives. The same power that dwelled in those women of faith dwells inside you today. You can resist any operation of death in any area of your life.

7. HOPE VERSUS HOPELESSNESS

The old life lacks genuine power, so those under it surrender easily to every challenge. People give up because there is no power to activate their desires. This happens because they are spiritually empty. On the other hand, In the new life we received, there is hope and there is a Shepherd. Consequently, our future is guaranteed and no matter the difficult situation, it is a matter of time, something positive will happen for our sake. We are a people of hope. This assurance is echoed in *Jeremiah 31:17*; *'And there is hope in thine end, saith the LORD, that thy children shall come again to their own border.'* That is, no matter how difficult a situation may appear to be, there is promotion at the end. There will be achievement of desires. Vision will speak, it is only a matter of time.

Job 14:7 says *'For there is hope of a tree, if it be cut down, that it will sprout again, and that the tender branch thereof will not cease.'* Your business may be down today but very soon, it will rise again. The righteous will never be defeated as long as he refuses to surrender. There is something good about to happen in your life. There is a shout of joy about to come out of your home. Something is about to happen in your favour. Job kept the fire of hope and at the end, he experienced restoration that was humanly impossible. In all his difficult situations, Job kept on saying:

Job 19:25
For I know that my redeemer liveth, and that he shall stand at the latter day upon the earth.

At the end, his redeemer arose for his restoration. May God fill your mouth with words of hope in Jesus' name.

8. NON-RENEWAL VERSUS RENEWAL

There is no renewal in the old life. Things diminish without renewal and fade away after a time. Positions fade away, blessings fade away. There is no power to renew strength. First love fades away without renewal. However, In the new life that we received, there is power that renews things. Strength can be renewed. Ideas can be renewed. Hope can be renewed. Wealth can be renewed. Our God always does new things. You can have a new beginning in the Lord Jesus. *Psalms 103:5* talks about a God *'Who satisfieth thy mouth with good things; so that thy youth is renewed like the eagle's.'*

That is you can remain strong always. You don't need to grow weaker and weaker. Your strength can be renewed. You can always be active without diminishing in vigour. *2 Corinthians 4:16* says *'For which cause we faint not; but though our outward man perish, yet the inward man is renewed day by day.'*

The above shows that as a new creature, you can remain spiritually strong throughout your days. You can always be on fire for God. It is possible for you to remain infallible in all your days because your inner man never diminishes. *Isaiah 40:31* assures thus: *'But they that wait upon the LORD shall renew their strength; they shall mount up with wings as eagles; they shall run, and not be weary; and they shall walk, and not faint.'*

As a new creature, there is a power inside of you that can keep you strong always. You can keep on trusting God as you used to do in the past. You can outrun your enemy in the race of life. You can reign in the midst of storm.

Job 17:9
The righteous also shall hold on his way, and he that hath clean hands shall be stronger and stronger.

You can be stronger and stronger. You can move from strength to strength in your career, vision, ministry etc. It is possible. May God keep you on top in all your days in Jesus' name.

9. EXHAUSTIBLE VERSUS INEXHAUSTIBLE

The source in the old life is exhaustible. It can run dry. It can run dry of idea, wisdom, riches, strength, help, hope etc. In the old life a rich man of today can become poor tomorrow. The leader of today can become a servant the next day. The helper can die in the old life. In the new life we received the source that is inexhaustible. It can never run dry. Our source is so rich such that after generations have drawn from it, there is still a great inheritance for the next generation. **Proverbs 13:22** affirms that *'A good man leaveth an inheritance to his children's children: and the wealth of the sinner is laid up for the just.'*

The provision of God always outlives the receiver. It should not finish during your own life. God wants your children to inherit blessings from you and pass it on to the next generation after them.

10. SEASONAL VERSUS SEASONLESS

The situation in the old life is season-controlled. If the economy of a nation is good, people prosper, otherwise, they suffer retardation. In the new life, our economy and situation are not season-controlled. We live beyond the season. We make profit in all seasons.

> **Zechariah 14:8**
> And it shall be in that day, that living waters shall go out from Jerusalem; half of them toward the former sea, and half of them toward the hinder sea: in summer and in winter shall it be.

Our source is not affected by the season and time. There is no bad time; all times are good. When God becomes your source, you will always be fruitful irrespective of the economy or political situation of where you live. As a new creature, don't accept the dictates of the economic situation of your country. Your source is in heaven and is not affected by the worldly situation. Wherever you live, your supply will locate you because it is made in heaven. May God lift you up above the situation of your country in Jesus' name.

Jeremiah 17:7-8 says *'Blessed is the man that trusteth in the LORD, and whose hope the LORD is. For he shall be as a tree planted by the waters, and that spreadeth out her roots by the river, and shall not see when heat cometh, but her leaf shall be green; and shall not be careful in the year of drought, neither shall cease from yielding fruit.'*

God designed you to be fruitful in all seasons. You should not have bad days; all days must be good for you. You should not wait for supposed good time to move into your destiny. The time is now. All time is good for you. You can get a job now. You can achieve your vision now. You can be totally healed now. It does not matter what the season of the world is, you have immunity against it. Arise and do great things now!

11. REALITY VERSUS SUPERNATURAL

The old life is a life of reality. It is controlled by senses and feelings. It operates by sight. If a situation does not appear good, then it is not good. The new life is a life of the supernatural. As a new creature of God, you were saved to live a life of the supernatural-a life that walks by faith, not by sight. There is no application of senses and feelings, but the spirit. Though in reality, a situation may not look good outside but to you, it is good. We see through the eyes of the spirit, not those of the body.

2 Corinthians 5:7
For we walk by faith, not by sight.

By sight, a situation may look bad but by faith, it is good. By sight, it may be a hopeless situation but by faith, there is hope. Your life should be controlled not by what you see but by what you believe. If you believe that you are a victor, then the battle that seems big before you will appear as nothing. If you believe that by the stripes of Jesus you were healed, then you should speak healing into your sick body. Allow what you believe to dictate your word, not what you see or feel. *2 Corinthians 4:13* expresses the faith thus *'We having the same spirit of faith, according as it is written, I believed, and therefore have I spoken; we also believe, and therefore speak.'*

Faith makes you to operate in the supernatural.

12. LOSING VERSUS WINNING

The old life is full of losses. Every member of the old life is a loser. They lose even the smallest battle because it is a life that of losses. The reason is because the members fight their own battle by themselves. In the new life we received, we are victors; always winning. The secret of our victory is that our God always fights our battles for us. Our God is a man of war and He is undefeatable. We have been given victory, so we don't need to strive for it again. Every battle you will ever face in your life has already been won for you as a new creature. According to *2 Chronicles 20:15*, the battle is of the Lord. As a new creature, your role in the battle of your life is to praise God, to motivate Him to fight for you.

1 Samuel 17:47 reveals thus: *'And all this assembly shall know that the LORD saveth not with sword and spear: for the battle is the LORD'S, and he will give you into our hands.'* David was not afraid of the mighty Goliath because he knew that the battle was not for him but the Lord's. You don't need to be afraid of any battle because you are not the one to fight it but your God. May you always win and may God arise and all His enemies troubling you be scattered in Jesus' name.

13. BONDAGE VERSUS LIBERTY

The old life is full of bondage and there is no freedom. No freedom of choice, vision, purpose, desires etc. It is full of enslavement. People do according to the dictates of their masters. They live under fear. Their lives are fear-controlled. In the new life, there is liberty. You are free to make choices. You have been empowered and positioned to live above fear and the dictates of the world.

> **2 Corinthians 3:17**
> Now the Lord is that Spirit: and where the Spirit of the Lord is, there is liberty.

As a new creature, you are free from the bondage of the law and human tradition. Your life can no more be ruled by what is permissible and not permissible in your family. You can no more be a partaker of family and generational sicknesses. You can no more participate in your family festivals and customs that dictate what to eat and do and what not to eat and do, to you. You are free from those demonic controls. You are only related to your earthly family by natural means but as a new creature your real family is heavenly. Your genetic composition has changed. Your family tree has changed. Your inheritance has changed. You can no longer accept family rules that control the level and attainment of success. It may be possible that there are certain evil that befall members of your family at certain stages of their lives, but you have been set free from such occurrence. You are a new specie.

The seeds of frustration and death were removed from your system the day you became a new creature. No more generational sicknesses and failures. Refuse to respect the evil that prevails in your earthly family. Nothing can harm you if you refuse to observe any family tradition and belief. You have been grafted to a new olive tree which is Jesus Christ. Those demonic spirits hitherto ruling your earthly family can no longer claim ownership over your life as you no longer belong to them. You have been set free; do not enter into any form of bondage again. Maintain your freedom and resist any empty threat from the enemy of your soul.

8

OUR NEW NAMES IN PRAYER

As a new creature you have been given a new name. Your old name came from the description of events of your life in the past. People use the situation in someone's life to describe him. The world will call barren those who are yet to have children, while those who lost a battle will be called failures. As a new creature, your name has changed. Your new names are formed from the heavenly identity, a new name given by God. As you pray these new names into your life, you will be seeing new things happening in your life in accordance with your heavenly identities.

Prayer by Prophetic Declaration According to the Biblical Names of Christians

I declare:

1. AS A FRIEND OF GOD (*John 15:15*)

I am a friend of God. I gain access into the knowledge of God. The secret of God shall dwell with me. I shall walk in the relational knowledge of God in Jesus name.

2. AS A CHOSEN ONE (*John 15:16*)

I have been chosen by God to be fruitful. I shall be fruitful in all my ways this year. My hands shall be fruitful, my legs shall be fruitful. My mind shall be fruitful, my brain shall be fruitful, and my spirit shall be fruitful. Every part of me shall be fruitful this year in Jesus name.

3. AS AN ORDAINED OF GOD (*Jeremiah 1:5*)

I have been set apart for God. I shall walk in the purpose of God and used by God this year. I shall not be used by man. I shall not be used by the devil. The world shall not use me. I shall only be used by God throughout this year in Jesus name.

4. AS A SERVANT OF GOD (*John 13:16*)

I am a servant of God. The Lord is my Master. Only God shall rule over my life. No other power shall be able to rule over me. I shall live under the dominion and authority of God only in Jesus name. The devil shall not gain control of my life in Jesus name.

5. AS A SON OF GOD (*Galatians 4:6*)

I am a son of God. I have an inheritance from God. This year, I shall enjoy my inheritance from God. Success is my inheritance, victory is my inheritance, healing is my inheritance, favour is my inheritance, prosperity is my inheritance, honour is my inheritance, I shall enjoy all my inheritance fully this year in Jesus name.

6. AS A GOD (*Psalms 82:6*)

I am a god. I am the representative of God. I operate in the authority of God. Whatever I bind shall be bound; whatever I lose shall be lose. Whatever I decree shall be established. Whatever I ask to come shall come; whatever I ask to go shall go in Jesus' name.

7. AS A VESSEL UNTO HONOUR (*2 Timothy 2:21*)

I am a vessel unto honour in the hands of God. God shall use me to bless nations this year. Through me, God shall heal people. Through me, God shall set the captives free in Jesus' name.

8. AS A CHRISTIAN (*Acts 11:26*)

I am a Christian. I walk as Jesus walked. I talk as Jesus talked. I act as Jesus acted. I do as Jesus did. I have the mind of Christ. The world shall see Christ in me this year in Jesus' name.

9. AS THE LIGHT (*Matthew 5:14*)

I am the light of the world. Wherever I go this year, darkness shall flee from my presence. Through me, the world shall receive understanding and the knowledge of God. I am the light of the world in Jesus name.

10. AS THE SALT OF THE WORLD (*Matthew 5:13*)

I am the salt of the world. The goodness of God dwells with me. Whoever has contact with me this year shall be saved. I am a carrier of God's goodness in Jesus' name.

11. AS THE RANSOMED OF THE LORD (*Isaiah 35:10*)

I am the ransomed of the lord. The lord has set me free from captivity. I have been set free from sickness, poverty, failure and every manner of evil. I am a free person in the Lord. No more bondage in Jesus' name.

12. AS THE RIGHTEOUS (*Matthew 13:43*)

I am the righteous of the Lord. I have overcome the accusations of the enemy. I have overcome condemnation of the enemy. No one can bring any charge against me. I am righteous. I am holy. I am a just man in the eye of the Lord. My accuser shall be put to shame forever in Jesus' name.

13. AS THE ELECT (*1 Peter 1:2*)

I am an elect of the Lord. I am God's favourite. I am a special person. This year, I shall enjoy special provisions from God. I shall enjoy special blessings from God. In all my ways, I shall receive special treatment in Jesus' name.

14. AS THE REDEEMED OF THE LORD (*Isaiah 51:11*)

I am the redeemed of the lord. I have been redeemed from death, destruction, all troubles, sin, and every manner of curses. No evil shall locate me this year in Jesus' name.

15. AS THE SAINT OF THE LORD (*Daniel 7:18*)

I am a saint of the most high God. I am pure. My spirit is pure. My soul is pure. My body is pure. My mind is pure. My heart is pure. My destiny is pure. My life is not contaminated and it will never be contaminated in Jesus' name.

16. AS AN AMBASSADOR OF GOD (2 *Corinthians 5:20*)

I am an ambassador of God. I speak for God. The word of God dwells within me. I represent God; I carry the glory of God. The presence of God is with me. Whoever sees me this year has seen God, in Jesus' name.

17. AS AN EPISTLE OF GOD (2 *Corinthians 3:3*)

I am the epistle of Jesus. The world shall read Jesus through me. My life shall minister Jesus to the world. My life shall bring the message of Jesus to this dying world. The world shall come to Jesus through the testimonies of my life this year in Jesus' name.

18. AS THE SUN (*Matthew 13:43*)

I am the sun. As no one can cover the glory of the sun, so shall no one be able to cover the glory of God in my life in Jesus' name.

19. AS THE BELIEVER OF GOD (*Acts 5:14*)

I am a believer of God. I believe in God. I believe in Jesus. I believe in the Holy Spirit. I believe the work of Trinity. My life shall manifest the works of the Trinity. I believe it and I receive it in Jesus' name.

20. AS A BELOVED OF GOD (*Romans 1:7*)

I am a beloved of God. God loves me. He will fight my battle for me. He will defend me. He will save me. He will watch over me. He will journey with me. I will enjoy God's care in all my ways in Jesus' name.

21. AS A CHILD OF ABRAHAM BY FAITH (*Galatians 3:7*)

I am a child of Abraham by faith. Whoever blesses me shall be blessed; whoever curses me shall be cursed in Jesus name.

22. AS A LIVELY STONE (*1 Peter 2:5*)

I am a lively stone. I am a living stone. I house God. The fullness of God dwells inside of me. The treasures of God dwell inside of me. There is nothing of the devil in me. I shall manifest God wherever I go in Jesus' name.

23. AS A TREE PLANTED BY THE RIVERS (*Psalms 1:3*)

I am a tree planted by the rivers of waters. I will always be prosperous. Whatever I put my hand into shall prosper greatly in Jesus' name. Every season shall favour me this year.

24. AS AN EAGLE (*Isaiah 40:31*)

I am an eagle. I shall soar like an eagle. I shall rise quickly and speedily this year. Every challenge that comes on my way this year shall lift me up in Jesus name.

25. AS MOUNT ZION (*Psalms 125:1-2*)

I am mount Zion, the city of the Lord. The Lord surrounds me always. I am unmovable, unshakeable and untouchable. The Lord of hosts is with me always in Jesus' Name.

26. AS A KING (*Revelation 1:6*)

I am a king. I have the dominion of a king. I have the authority of a king. I rule. I shall reign in life. I will live in dominion and I shall never be ruled by any evil force. Every created thing shall obey my command this year in Jesus name.

27. AS A ROYAL PRIESTHOOD (*1 Peter 2:9*)

I am a royal priesthood. I make sacrifice unto the Lord. All my sacrifice shall be accepted by God this year. The Lord shall show favour to all my sacrifice of praise, thanksgiving and adoration. Whatever I offer unto the Lord shall receive God's blessings this year in Jesus' name.

28. AS A STAR (*Daniel 12:3*)

I am a star. The Lord has made me a star to my generation. I shall shine in all my ways. I shall shine in my place of work. I shall shine in my marriage. I shall shine in my ministry. I shall shine everywhere and in everything in Jesus' name.

29. AS A PROPHET (*Ezekiel 37:4*)

I am a prophet. Therefore I prophesy concerning my life that:

- a. all the Egyptians I see today in my life, I shall see them no more in Jesus' name;
- b. all the dry bones of my life shall come alive today in Jesus' name;
- c. all is well with me throughout this year and all the years of my life in Jesus name;
- d. before I pray, answers shall locate me this year in Jesus' name; and
- e. I shall live under open heavens throughout this year in Jesus name.

30. AS ONE WHO HAS SPOKEN TO THE LORD'S EARS

I have spoken to the Lord's ears and according to His promises, He shall answer my prayers. *'Say unto them, As truly as I live, saith the LORD, as ye have spoken in mine ears, so will I do to you'* (**Numbers 14:28**).

Father, I thank you because as I have spoken in your ears today, so you will do to and for me in Jesus' name. Amen.

BOOKS FROM THE SAME AUTHOR

The New Creature

Words That Heal

Building a Glorious Home

The Winning Dose

This book, and all other books from the same author, are available at Christian bookstores and distributors worldwide.
They can also be obtained through online retail partners such as Amazon or by contacting the author on the address below.

Contacts:
21-23 Stokescroft
Bristol BS1 3PY
United Kingdom

E-mail:
kkasali@yahoo.com

www.ingramcontent.com/pod-product-compliance
Lightning Source LLC
Chambersburg PA
CBHW072048290426
44110CB00014B/1592